Gender, Change & Society: 2

Gender and Career in Science and Engineering

Gender and Career in Science and Engineering

Julia Evetts

Taylor & Francis
Publishers since 1798

UK   Taylor & Francis Ltd, 1 Gunpowder Sq., London EC4A 3DE
USA   Taylor & Francis Inc., 1900 Frost Road, Suite 101, Bristol, PA 19007

First published 1996

**A Catalogue Record for this book is available from the British
Library**

ISBN 0 7484 0250 0 (cloth)
ISBN 0 7484 0251 9 (paper)

**Library of Congress Cataloguing-in-Publication Data are
available on request**

Typeset in 10/12 pt Times Roman
by Best-set Typesetter Ltd., Hong Kong

Printed in Great Britain by SRP Ltd, Exeter

For
Dave

Acknowledgments

I wish to express my thanks to all colleagues who have given support, encouragement, comment and advice while this book was being planned and written. Colleagues in the School of Social Studies of the University of Nottingham have provided cover for some of my departmental responsibilities during a semester of study leave. Colleagues at Nottingham and in other universities, and some in other countries, have given helpful advice on particular ideas and themes.

Special thanks are due to Robert Dingwall for time, space and support, which have been vital in enabling me to develop my ideas, and for comment and advice which have encouraged me to extend them. Thanks are due to Michael King for stimulating my interests in scientists, to my husband, Dave, for being an engineer, and to Victoria and Paul who might yet become organizational scientists. A particular debt of gratitude is due to Linda Poxon who has prepared the manuscript. Linda's efficiency, reliability, experience and skill enable me to overcome the difficulties which a strain injury to my right hand and arm continually present. Without her hard work and dedication, very little of my research would ever reach publication.

I also wish to express my sincere gratitude to the scientists and engineers who were the respondents in the careers history study. They gave their time and shared their experiences. I hope I have been able accurately to convey at least some of those experiences. Any faults in the manuscript are, of course, my own.

Julia Evetts

Contents

Introduction

This book sets out to explore the themes and issues which are relevant to understanding the experience of career of a particular group of professional workers. These workers are graduate (or equivalent) scientists and engineers employed in large industrial organizations. For professional scientists and engineers, defined as 'persons employed in technical work for which the normal qualification is a degree in science, maths or engineering' (McRae, Devine and Lakey, 1991, p. 7), there is still a growing demand for such personnel in Britain. Manufacturing industries anticipate a growth of 28 per cent in the employment of science and engineering professionals, while service industries expect a growth of 128 per cent (IER, 1988).

This particular group of professional workers, like others, has experienced enormous technological changes in their work in the 1980s and the effects of these changes have been discussed (Gershuny, 1983; Daniel, 1987; McLoughlin and Clark, 1988). There have been other large-scale changes in the industrial organization for which they work, as global competition, economic restructuring, deregulation and internal budgetary devolutions have required major rationalizations in production and distribution processes. This book also examines organizational processes, change and restructuring as major influences on professional careers.

An additional focus for the book, and for the analysis, is gender as a variable in career experiences and organizational processes. There are large gender differences within the professions of science and engineering. For example, Carter and Kirkup (1990) estimated that in 1986, only 4.6 per cent of professional engineers working in industry were women. During the 1980s in Britain, attempts were made to address the gender imbalances in science and engineering occupations. In 1984, the Women into Science and Engineering (WISE) campaign was established, promoted by the Equal Opportunities Commission and the Engineering Council, which resulted in numerous projects at both national and local levels. This campaign, like others (see McRae, Devine and Lakey, 1991), has heightened awareness and resulted in some numerical improvements. A survey of entrants into science and engineering degree courses suggested the proportion of women had increased to 12 per cent in 1987/8 (Engineering Council, quoted in McRae, Devine and

Lakey, 1991, p. 9). This proportion is expected to increase further, indicating an upward trend, even though it is an increase from a very low base.

There is still considerable scope for increases in the recruitment of women technologists and scientists into industry. McRae, Devine and Lakey (1991, p. 10), reporting the results of Elias and Rigg (Eds, 1990), show that although women made up 27 per cent of the new graduates recruited by the private sector, they made up only 17 per cent of those recruited to research and development posts and 18 per cent of those recruited to production and engineering. However, if considerable energy is being devoted to the recruitment of women into (professional) science and engineering, it is important to examine what happens to those women who have already entered. It is necessary to ask whether there are significant gender differences in professional careers in engineering and science in industry.

In sociological research, the concept of career has had a long and chequered history. Early research focused on organizations; careers were analysed as the processes by which organizations renewed themselves (Gunz, 1989). Research on careers in the 1950s and 1960s focused on organizational career structures and ladders and, as a result, the notions of progress and promotion came to be attached to the concept of career. Thus, Wilensky (1960, p. 127) defined career as 'a succession of related jobs, arranged in a hierarchy of prestige, through which persons move in an ordered predictable sequence'. He wanted to confine the use of the term 'career' to occupations located within organizations with hierarchical bureaucratic career structures. Slocum also defined career in a similar way: 'an occupational career may be defined for this discussion as an ordered sequence of development extending over a period of years and involving progressively more responsible roles within an occupation' (Slocum, 1966, p. 5). Thus the notion of progress within organizations and professions, in regular, successive stages, and of movement into jobs with increasing responsibility came to be attached to the term career. Careers could only be pursued where there were hierarchically arranged promotion positions, usually in bureaucratic organizational structures, through which position-holders were able to move in regular and successive stages, achieving promotion to more responsible and more highly paid posts. So, in organizational terms, the civil service and the teaching profession had career structures since they had formalized ladders of recognized posts and positions but not usually a factory employing manual workers.

Later, researchers shifted the focus to the study of career routes. In these cases, employees were the units rather than the organization and a 'career' was the succession of posts and positions through which employees moved during their working lives. Careers were how employees had moved through and between positions: the paths, the routes and the terminuses that were constructed and developed. In this context Brown (1982) distinguished between organizational careers (where advancement was achieved within a single employing organization) and occupational careers (where employees move from employer to employer in developing their careers).

Alongside this research on organizational careers, a second stream was developing based on the idea of the subjective career. In this research the emphasis was on how individual actors influence and develop their own social frameworks and social worlds in formal organizations. Hughes (1937) had identified a 'subjective career' which consisted of individuals' own changing perspectives towards their careers: how employees actually experienced 'having a career'. For Stebbins (1970), a subjective career was the actor's interpretation of events which demonstrated that different kinds of performance could be regarded as career 'success'. In this line of development, the concept of career was not only applied to paid work. Thus women could have a career in the context of the family; and deviants (Becker, 1963), psychiatric patients (Goffman, 1968) and prisoners (Taylor and Cohen, 1972) have been analysed as 'having a career' and as a 'process of becoming'.

When the subjective career concept was applied in the analysis of paid working careers, findings were significantly different from those arising from the study of organizational career ladders. The subjective career was not necessarily a smooth, unilinear development involving the successive movements, promotions and increased responsibilities of organizational careers. By concentrating on how people actually experienced their work and their careers, subjective careers could be very different from the organizational focus on people-flow and managerial renewal and replacement. The subjective career focused on individuals' experiences; how they saw the constraints and opportunities; how constraints and opportunities were negotiated and managed; how individuals perceived the problems and the possibilities, the influences, the turning-points, the key events and decisions.

In the analysis of subjective careers there was no prior assumption of promotion and progress, nor did the subjective career have to be centred solely on developments in the paid work sphere. This interpretation of career, as synonymous with a life-history, offered the possibilities of studying women's as well as men's careers and of opening up career structures to the influence of workers' objectives and intentions for their careers.

During the 1980s the issue of gender differences in careers came to prominence. Researchers made use of feminist concepts as well as ideas from the sociology of occupations and the professions in order to explore and attempt to account for the substantial gender differences in careers. For a time, researchers interested in women's careers had an uneasy relationship with feminist writers since their concerns were with women who were relatively privileged. Such women were receiving well-paid salaries; many could afford their own transport and pay for help with housework, childcare and responsibilities for elderly relatives; their occupations were secure and their careers were safe, if unspectacular. Compared with their less-privileged sisters, it was difficult to argue that the position of such women needed different explanatory theories and concepts compared with career men. It was probably not until the 1980s, when the statistics of women's minority position, ghettoization and marginalization in careered occupations and professions became more widely recognized and acknowledged (Silverstone and Ward, 1980; Spencer and Podmore, 1987), that researchers began to develop their own ideas and concepts to explore the issue of women and career.

For a time, the issue of women's careers in employment was high on political and social agendas. In Britain the report of the Hansard Society Commission (1990) was concerned about the lack of women in top positions in public service, in corporate management and in key areas of influence such as the media, universities and trade unions. In 1991 the public campaign 'Opportunity 2000' attracted a great deal of media attention for its objectives to increase the quantity and proportion of women's participation in higher levels of management in public and private work organizations. More recently, in the current period of economic recession, the momentum behind these initiatives has been slowed. It is usually only in more favourable economic circumstances that progress is made on social initiatives such as equal opportunities at work.

For a number of years now women have been entering occupations and professions which traditionally have been perceived as men's work. In Britain, the Sex Discrimination Act 1975 made both direct and indirect discrimination on the grounds of sex unlawful and the professions have seen increasing numbers of women achieving the educational qualifications necessary for initial entry. Gender differences still exist in numbers entering particular professions: and engineering and science are critical cases in this respect. However, the focus of interest has now shifted to what happens to women who *have* entered such areas of work. Promotion and progress for women, and gender differences in careers, are currently matters of interest and concern particularly for professional women themselves. As problems over gender differences in initial entry have eased, attention has focused on gender and promotion in professional careers.

Professional careers in engineering and science are mostly constructed in organizations, as distinct from professional firms and small or large practices. In organizational contexts, both industrial and service, senior positions result from regular promotion progress upwards through organizational career ladders. It is also the case that senior positions in organizations involve management. Promotion in engineering and science careers in organizations necessitates moving from doing the actual engineering and scientific work to managing others who are doing it.

This career route out of engineering into management has posed a problem of professional identity for engineers (Finniston, 1980). The notion of their *particular* expertise is in any case unclear since their knowledge base and skills are often wide and very diverse. Similar problems exist for professional scientists working in industrial organizations, since their professional identities have usually been derived from academic scientists working in universities or research institutes. For both engineers and scientists, therefore, when career and promotion necessitate a move into management, the problem of professional identity is intensified.

How, then, are the careers of scientists and engineers developed in large industrial organizations? Are there any significant gender differences in such careers? These are the fundamental questions addressed in this book, along with others concerning career experiences, organizational processes and change as well as continuity in career contexts and career outcomes. The first chapter develops a general framework for the analysis of careers. Three dimensions of career (culture, structure and action) are outlined and explained and the gender differences are indicated. The dimensions are illustrated and related to a developing research tradition on gender and careers in professional and organizational contexts. Importantly, these dimensions are closely interrelated and mutually supportive aspects of careers and of gender differences in them.

The second chapter is concerned with the categories of 'scientist' and 'engineer' as professional and organizational workers. It includes analysis of some of the main theoretical issues which researchers have considered fundamental in determining the position and role of such workers. The chapter examines the concepts of class, profession, organization and control over scientific and technological knowledge and expertise. It explores how gender needs to be incorporated alongside these concepts in order to further develop understanding about industrial scientists and engineers as categories of professional workers.

The careers history respondents themselves are introduced in Chapter 3 which provides background data on this group of women and men, scientists and engineers. The chapter summarizes the characteristics of the respondents and gives details about the two industrial organizations for which they worked. The careers history methodology and the epistemology for the study are also explained.

The remaining chapters make use of the data supplied by the careers history respondents in the exploration of particular career and gender themes. Chapter 4 considers the educational experiences of this group of women and men. Their choices of 'A'-level subjects, careers advice, mentoring and first experiences of industrial work are examined. Any differences between the scientists and engineers, the women and the men, are explored. Aspects of their work, their work cultures and identities are examined in Chapter 5. Again, any differences in experiences between the scientists and engineers, the women and men, are identified and discussed.

The combination of the career with personal and private lives is discussed in Chapter 6 where a classification of different patterns of resolution of such responsibilities is proposed. The differences between the women and men are identified and the influence of policies within the organizations are assessed. This chapter also considers other aspects of the combination of work and private lives, such as childcare arrangements and the increasing significance of dual-career partnerships where both partners work in the same or similar fields. These career partnerships are perceived to give rise to additional forms of career competition, this time within families rather than organizations.

Chapters 7 and 8 deal with related themes. Chapter 7 considers the issue of promotion in the organization for professional scientists and engineers. The influence of organizational processes, promotion structures and career ladders is assessed here together with the variety and variation in individual solutions. The differences in the resolutions of the women and men in the careers history group are examined, such as their different attitudes to promotion and their different experiences of difficulties. In Chapter 8, the particular problems which management presents for careers in science and engineering are explored. Some of the cultural dimensions of management in organizations are highlighted. There is a growing literature on gender and management and the particular problems which women encounter in the competition for, and operation of, managerial posts is assessed and reviewed in the light of the experiences of the careers history respondents.

Finally, Chapter 9 summarizes some of the ideas and themes which are important in the analysis of the experience of career in professional science and engineering in large industrial organizations. The interrelated themes of culture, structure and action dimensions of career are used to summarize and comment on the main aspects of continuity and change in the gender experiences of career. The organizations themselves are considered and their current changes are assessed as changing structural contexts for careers in science and engineering. This involves an exploration of how career, gender, management and organization are interacting to produce new, as well as old, career patterns and forms of occupational segregation.

Chapter 1

Gender and Career: the Culture, Structure and Action Dimensions of Change

This book is concerned with the careers of scientists and engineers working in large industrial organizations. It will attempt to illuminate and explore the factors which shape such careers. The primary focus will be the career experiences of individuals and the career processes in organizations. Throughout the analysis, gender constitutes a critical variable and gender differences in the experiences of career will be examined. Aspects of change in experiences and in processes in organizations will also be considered, alongside any aspects of stability, continuity and reproduction.

The careers that are the focus of attention are those of women and men in organizations. They are professionals in the sense that they are graduates, or the equivalent, and they are also, or most will be, members of professional scientific associations or chartered engineering institutions. Yet, as professionals, their careers are being constructed and developed in industrial organizations. They are employees and their careers are defined and determined by organization-specific promotion ladders and organizational needs and requirements. Such promotion ladders are defined in terms of merit, additional qualifications, achievements, experience and career potential. The lower levels of organizational promotion ladders are frequently criterion-referenced, which allow large numbers of scientists and engineers to achieve initial promotion in the early stages of their careers. Subsequent promotion, at the higher levels of organizations, are more often by invitation only and where more subjective assessments are made of the matching of individuals' promotion potential and organizational requirements. The linking of qualifications and promotions gives legitimacy to the meritocratic ideology of organizations; qualifications form the prerequisites for merit-based systems of promotion and career development. Qualifications also bestow competence on practitioners which is of great significance to maintaining the ideology of professionalism (Crompton and Sanderson, 1990).

In promotion terms, qualified individuals can develop linear careers in organizations where they achieve regular and successive promotion upwards in hierarchical career structures. Beyond a particular point in organizational career ladders, positions involve increasing management responsibility. Alternatively, qualified individuals can continue at practitioner levels in organizations. Some organizations have also developed professional promotion ladders, parallel to managerial positions, to be able to reward and encourage individuals who are developing professional, rather than managerial, careers. Many qualified women develop occupational careers which might include extended periods at practitioner levels, perhaps during part-time employment. Crompton and Sanderson (1990) noted that part-time work is not considered relevant to the linear careers that are developed in organizational (and professional) contexts. It is in respect of linear promotion that women's careers, compared with men's, are at a disadvantage. The statistical demonstration of women's disadvantaged position in promotion terms in organizations and professions is easy to reveal (e.g. Evetts, 1994a). Men predominate at the higher promotion levels of organizations and professions and 'organizational hierarchies are not sympathetic to women' (Crompton and Sanderson, 1990, p. 71).

This chapter considers a framework of analysis which is used and developed in the chapters that follow. In the analysis of change or continuity in career experiences, the dimensions of culture, structure and action constitute different, though closely interrelated, aspects of career (Evetts, 1992). These three dimensions of career and career experiences are outlined and illustrated. This classification of the dimensions of career is used as an heuristic device, however, to assist the presentation and review of what is, in fact, a diverse and complex literature. Thus, aspects of career are grouped in dimensions according to the theoretical model employed and often also the different research models utilized. It is not claimed that researchers are proponents of one of these dimensions to the exclusion of others. Rather it is that different kinds of analysis, incorporating different kinds of data, are likely to yield explanations which are either cultural, structural or subjective accounts of career experiences.

In the review of the dimensions of career that follows, the gender aspects of career experiences are highlighted. Analysis has tended to focus on explaining the stability, continuation and reproduction of gender differences in careers. In reviewing these different dimensions it will be shown that change is underemphasized but is nevertheless an important, constant and continuous feature of career experiences. Each section ends by considering some of the most prominent aspects of change. In this way it is argued that some combination of cultural, structural and action dimensions of change in organizations provides an improved explanatory model for the analysis of women's careers as well as men's.

Cultural dimensions of careers

In explanations focusing on cultural factors, researchers consider the belief systems and controlling social institutions that influence occupational choice as well as an analysis of gender differences in attributes, ways of working and style. Explanations in terms of culture emphasize the controlling notions of femininity and masculinity, of what it means to be a woman and a man and on the ideology of the family that influences such notions. In such explanations, data might include analysis and often deconstruction of belief systems and controlling ideologies in contemporary society. These ideological aspects are illustrated first. Gender differences in style are then examined. The section ends by outlining the changes in cultural belief systems that are affecting women's and men's experiences of career.

Gender and family ideologies

The concept of ideology is used in this context to refer to the cultural belief systems that influence behaviour by means of commonsense notions of what is 'natural' as well as through moral precepts of what is good, right and appropriate. The issue of gender and ideology has been addressed both in respect of masculinity (Seidler, 1989; Cohen, 1990; Roper and Tosh, (Eds) 1991) and earlier in respect of femininity (Klein, 1972; Kuhn and Wolpe, 1978). Feminist theory has been concerned with questions of gender identity, how gender is transmitted and learned and how the child develops a sense of gendered self. The constraints and contradictions of women's gender identities have been discussed in some detail (e.g. Farganis, 1986). Writers on motherhood (Badinter, 1982; Brannen and Moss, 1991) have noted historical changes and have described the costs involved in the current practice of women-raised children both for the women involved (Rich, 1976) and for the children, especially as this affects their sense of self and others (Chodorow, 1978).

For boys there is an assumption that work will constitute a fundamental part of their adult identities. Occupation is a vital aspect of self, and work identity has been critical in individuals' feelings of satisfaction and self-worth. This has caused difficulties for young men entering adulthood in an age of widespread unemployment (Allatt, 1986; Allen, 1986; Breakwell *et al.*, 1984; Breakwell, 1986), as well as for men facing redundancy or entering retirement. For those in work, however, expectations for careers have been superimposed on to work identities in a complementary way for middle-class non-manual and professional workers. Such workers *expect* to be promoted after gaining experience and skills, either in the context of their current work organization, perhaps through relocating, or through moving to another organization.

Marriage and fatherhood in no way contradict these work and career expectations. In some families, wives work to support and provide essential back-up services for their husbands' developing careers. Either by performing all the childcare and domestic responsibilities or by fulfilling other work-related duties for their husbands (Finch, 1983), wives work 'behind the scenes' to develop two-person, single-career strategies (Evetts, 1994b, pp. 54–7). Marriage and fatherhood have not tended to provide career dilemmas for men seeking promotion or even relocation, although there is some indication that men are beginning to experience higher levels of family/career conflict

(Thompson, Thomas and Maier, 1992). Thus, as women are also beginning to develop careers, some men's expectations of complete partnership support in their own careers might need to change.

For women there is no complementarity between work, career and family expectations; instead there is complete and increasing contradiction. There is an assumption for girls that motherhood will feature somewhere in their future and this is internalized in girls as they grow up (Chodorow 1978). Sharpe (1984) and Griffin (1985) have argued that in spite of a broadening in attitudes and increased opportunities in education and work, being feminine still involves marriage and motherhood. These remain central to girls' expectations as shown by research into their perceptions of their feminine role (Sharpe, 1976) and the culture of femininity (McRobbie, 1978). Gender identity, which includes being a 'good' mother, is critically important in women's sense of satisfaction and feelings of self-worth.

Throughout this century, the absence of many women from public life and paid work had resulted in them being defined and described and indeed in seeing themselves principally in terms of their family relationships, as someone's daughter, wife or mother. Today, paid work has assumed a more central and continuous place in most women's lives. The large majority of women now engage in paid work for a substantial proportion of their adult lives. The break for childcare is still common but even here more women than ever before are returning to work after completing their maternity leave (McRae, 1991). For women in careered occupations, the numbers returning are even higher than for women workers in general (Martin and Roberts, 1984). The greatest numbers of women returning to work are in professional and managerial grade occupations, where about 60 per cent of mothers with children under five are in employment (McRae, 1991). In this way, continuing in paid work offers these women an opportunity to develop and retain a work identity separate from their home and family.

The beliefs incorporated in the cultural dimensions of femininity and family, masculinity and career, continue to be powerful controlling forces in women's and men's working lives. Such ideologies affect the ways in which women and men choose an occupation or profession, decide to balance paid and unpaid work, and their sense of satisfaction with themselves as partners, parents, adult children and professional or career workers. Against such ideological forces, the linear career which enables men to achieve promotion and increased salary, and the practitioner career which enables women to combine paid and unpaid professional work while avoiding promotion, would seem highly rational choices (Brannen and Moss, 1991). For a man to pursue a linear career and compete for promotion is expected, normal and good, but a woman has to consciously oppose the ideological dictates of family and motherhood as well as the cultural controls of what it means to be feminine. Such powerful ideological forces have had a clear, controlling effect on women's career aspirations and achievements.

Such cultural dimensions of career continue to differentially affect the career experiences of women and men. The experiences of the scientists and engineers in this study are used to illustrate the career impacts of cultural factors and the differential effects on the women and men. For the women scientists and engineers, the reconciliation of public and private responsibilities, promotion and particularly management in their career, presented difficulties as well as opportunities. Such difficulties were experienced as well as sometimes resolved in different ways.

Gender styles

In this kind of analysis, questions have centred on whether gender differentiates working practices including management styles or whether gender is relatively insignificant in work cultures. Early research on women in professional and managerial work had been concerned to demonstrate 'no difference' in leadership styles and task performance (see the summary of such work in Marshall, 1984, pp. 14–17). Shakeshaft (1987) argued that such a strategy was essential in the 1960s and 1970s in order to refute the biases and prejudices which claimed that women were less effective than men in promotion positions.

In the 1980s, feminists began to pursue a different strategy which *emphasized* gender differences and gave prominence to female (in contrast to male) attributes. In developing this strategy, the work of Gilligan (1982) and her examination of gender differences in thinking and moral perception have been very influential. A developmental psychologist, Gilligan argued that women use a 'different voice' from men in talking about their relationships with others and in their conceptions of moral priorities. Women's voices speak of an 'ethic of care' which comes out of their social experiences and is in contrast with the 'ethic of justice' which is essentially male.

Gilligan's analysis has been challenged and the ahistorical character of some of her assertions has been criticized (Scott, 1986). However, the works of Gilligan and other feminist writers (e.g. Hartsock, 1983) were used increasingly during the 1980s to support arguments about gender differences in style in the conduct of administrative, managerial and professional work. Efforts were made to analyse the existence of a specifically female work culture. Such a culture was seen to emphasize collegiality (rather than hierarchy), caring and sensitivity in relationships (rather than authority) and had a different perception of priority and good practice. It was also suggested that such a female work culture was in many respects superior for clients, customers, work colleagues and workers themselves (e.g. Gray, 1987).

This strategy of asserting difference, rather than sameness, helped to shift the focus away from women's deficiencies in career terms on to their strengths. Marshall (1984), for example, talked about women managers taking communal and relatedness values with them into companies. Some of the effects she perceived to be a perspective on connectedness and an acceptance of affiliation and cooperation (in contrast to individual competition) as an alternative and improved means of getting work done. However, the dilemma for women seeking promotion in organizations and professions remains. If work, the professions, industry and organizations, as presently constituted, are ones where individual attributes and career competitiveness constitute what is recognized as promotion potential, then women who want to achieve career promotion will be required to meet such expectations.

The sameness/difference argument represents an unresolved dilemma in feminist thinking (Pateman, 1988; Bacchi, 1990). Thus to argue that women are 'the same' as men is inappropriate since this is to measure women against a male-defined standard. But to argue that women are essentially different is hazardous since one consequence is simplistic stereotyping by gender. More recent discussions of androgyny have emphasized the balancing of male and femaleness in all individuals. It is also highly risky for feminists to allow the values of rationality, objectivity and justice to be associated with maleness and thereby denied to women. It could be argued that the constant reassertion of female difference will, in the longer term, be unhelpful and is likely to reproduce aspects of occupational and career segregation. Thus, by reaffirming gender differences, women might continue to avoid the competitive world of organizational career, thereby leaving the real structures of power and influence to men. Alternatively, if women have to adopt so-called 'masculine' attributes in order to succeed, then stereotypical notions of gender difference will continue to handicap women's promotion progress. Either of these possibilities would constitute the reproduction of existing structures of gender relations and job segregation in careers in organizations.

Aspects of change in cultural influences

In general, then, explanations that focus on cultural attributes and ideological constraints have been prominent and persuasive in accounting for gender differences in careers. The arguments are complex and only a brief indication has been possible here. Cultural aspects present different kinds of problems for women's and men's careers. If the cultural qualities and characteristics expected of women and men are different, whether as a result of nature and/or socialization, then different occupational roles will be the likely outcome. Women will *prefer* certain kinds of occupation, in particular those which involve caring, nurturing and cooperative work roles. As a result, women will seek the satisfaction of helping others in their chosen fields and avoid the potentially hostile, competitive and assertive areas of promotion in the organizational career. Such cultural expectations might constitute part of the explanation for gender differences in careers.

It is necessary to acknowledge, however, that there have been some changes in controlling ideologies and in cultural expectations. Images of family are now diverse and variable. Single parenthood is the fastest growing family form (Social Trends, 1994) and weekend-only partnerships are an increasing pattern, particularly for dual-career couples. Associated changes (sometimes perceived as causal!) have occurred in women's attachment to paid work and in their career ambitions. Women now *expect* to be in paid work for the large majority of their adult lives (Dex, 1988). The break for childcare, which in the past often marked the end of the paid-work career for most married women, is now frequently limited only to paid maternity leave. Some women who are educated, trained and experienced in their occupations are showing more reluctance to develop practitioner careers (Crompton and Sanderson, 1990). Instead they want to compete for the higher salaried, managerial positions in organizations and professions. In general there is more variation (more choice?) in women's career ambitions and expectations.

There is also more variety in women's management of public and private work responsibilities. In the 1980s, researchers concentrated on the problems of the 'double shift' as women struggled to combine their paid work with their unpaid domestic and caring responsibilities. Indeed, McRae (1986) noted a tendency for career women to compensate for their 'unusual' occupational behaviour by retaining responsibility and control of housework and care duties. New divisions of domestic labour are beginning to emerge, however, as in some partnerships both partners are developing careers. Gregson and Lowe (1994) noted new forms of 'between partners' domestic divisions of labour as a result of the employment of waged domestic labour.

Difficulties remain and must not be underestimated. The lack of childcare and care for the elderly facilities which are perceived as appropriate in Britain cause practical problems as well as career difficulties for working women and men, though particularly for women. The criticisms voiced particularly by older generations continue to cause guilt and insecurity for many working women although no criticisms are applied to career men who neglect their private responsibilities. Women who, in their career actions and behaviour, seem to challenge gender stereotypes will always be perceived as odd, as different (or even deficient) in essential aspects of femininity, caring and relatedness. They will be admired by a few but criticized by other women, as well as men, in their attempts to break new ground. Men who are career achievers are admired and applauded for their promotion success. Such powerful ideological forces and cultural expectations have had, and continue to have, a clear, controlling effect on women's and men's career aspirations and expectations.

It is necessary to acknowledge, however, that controlling ideologies and cultural expectations have shifted and that there are important aspects of change as well as of continuity. The expectations surrounding motherhood have perhaps changed most: the 'good' mother is no longer required to completely abandon other aspects of the self. Notions of partnership have also altered significantly as men (as well as women) are required to acknowledge that their partners also have careers. The experiences of the women and men scientists and engineers in this study illustrate some of these aspects of culture change as well as continuity. When the focus is change, as well as stability and continuity, other aspects need to be incorporated in explanations of gender differences in career.

Structural dimensions of careers

When research focuses on actual work organizations and professions and women's and men's positions in different organizations are compared, perhaps using company records and data on occupational distribution, a different kind of explanation often results. In this case the focus is on organizational processes, as well as on the operation of internal and local labour markets. These are important influences on all careers but they differentially affect the careers of women and men. Again these will be examined in turn, before the outlining of changes in the structural factors affecting careers.

Professional and organizational processes

These explanations examine the different impact that certain professional and organizational processes have on women's and men's careers. Bourne and Wikler (1982) described the 'discriminatory environment' and the 'maleness' of the professions. Witz (1992) analysed the professional practices of social closure, using material drawn from the emerging medical division of labour in the late nineteenth and early twentieth centuries. There have been conceptual debates about 'organizational cultures' (e.g. Morgan, 1986) and organizational power structures (Clegg, 1989) which might be factors affecting the patterns of gendered employment. Pringle (1989) and Hearn *et al.* (Eds, 1989) have discussed 'organizational sexuality' as an explanatory factor. Also, Collins' (1981) and Pfeffer's (1989) accounts were examinations of the 'political' construction of careers where the resources of workers and the politics of groups within organizations were examined in order to explain how careers were constructed.

The heightened awareness of gender issues has resulted in increased access by women to some professional and organizational positions. But, as Podmore and Spencer (1986, p. 44) have maintained, the 'stacking up' of women in particular sectors or 'ghettos' of organizations and professions has tended to emphasize rather than reduce the divisions between men's and women's work.

There has recently been growing interest in the ways in which gender and bureaucratic organizational processes interrelate and interact. In an edited collection, Savage and Witz (1992) have reviewed the theoretical developments which have resulted in gender and organizations having a prominent place in contemporary social theory. From the early focus on *bureaucratic* organization, feminists moved the discussion to how those bureaucracies are gendered. The concept of career enables the gender/organization paradigm to be analysed. The notion of the bureaucratic linear career, in contrast to practitioner careers, still has considerable explanatory mileage (Crompton and Le Feuvre, 1992; Savage, 1992a). It also enables the examination of specific types of gender configuration in complex industrial and service organizations to be undertaken. The cultural contradictions experienced by women in career positions in the professions and in management have also been a common theme in this structuralist research literature (Hearn *et al.*, Eds, 1989; Cockburn, 1991; Davidson and Cooper, 1992; Evetts, Ed., 1994a).

Other researchers have focused on the introduction of equal opportunities policies in work organizations and how organizational structures and hierarchies have responded to such policies. Cockburn (1991) evaluated the part played by men in diverting and resisting feminist change in four large organizations (a retail organization, a government department, a local authority and a trade union). Knight and Pritchard (1994) were surprised and disappointed by the lack of support and encouragement which their work on women's development programmes at Thorn Home Electronics International received from senior managers. Halford (1992) outlined the difficulties of pursuing equal opportunities policies within gendered organizations such as local government. In general, researchers have concluded that organizational structures have been either unaffected or have adapted and incorporated such policies with no significant changes in the gender distribution of organizational positions.

In this study, aspects of organizational processes will be considered in terms of the different consequences for the careers of women and men scientists and engineers. In particular, subsequent chapters examine the effects of bureaucracy in large organizations, the results of supposedly merit-based promotion systems and the processes whereby organizational careers become gendered.

Research of this kind has increased understanding, therefore, about the operation of gender systems in organizations and professions. The focus has tended to be on reproduction, however, and how aspects of change have been incorporated without any significant effects for women's careers. The emphasis on processes has also tended to minimize the influence of actors' choice and the consequent variations in careers. The analysis of the reproduction of gender and organizational systems, in emphasizing determinants, takes no account of untidy contradictions, of the differences between professions and work places, or of the possibilities for change both by individuals and work organizations themselves. Such differences between places of work are the focus of explanations in the next section.

Internal labour markets

The characteristics of the internal labour market for particular professional and occupational groups differentially affect the distribution of career opportunities for women and men. It is through the occupational culture of particu-

15

lar work and through the generalized acceptance of certain procedures and processes for controlling and managing promotion in that work, that internal labour markets or career opportunities or constraints are created. A gendered internal labour market is formed when a career structure emerges whereby some members (men) can progress and achieve promotion in the career whereas others (women) are left in practitioner/occupational positions.

There is a considerable body of evidence that women are excluded from career positions in the internal labour markets of organizations and professions (Kanter, 1977; Collinson and Knights, 1986; Crompton and Sanderson, 1990). Different occupations use different processes, however, rendering different internal labour markets distinctive. One way is through gender differentiated recruitment where men and women train and apply for different jobs. Savage (1992b) explored this in respect of work and careers in banking in the first half of this century. There are other mechanisms, however, which have been receiving increased attention as more women have been training for and recruited on to the bottom levels of career ladders. Bourdieu (1986) has talked about the 'habitus' and Atkinson (1983) the 'indeterminate' knowledge of professional and organizational life. Using these concepts, the problem for women is not their human capital: that is, women's investment in technical knowledge and expertise. Rather, the problem is professional contact, style and legitimacy: 'their perceived failure to behave in ways which reveal their mastery of the indeterminate: that is, their failure to share the habitus' (Atkinson and Delamont, 1990, p. 107).

Along similar lines, the mechanisms of networking, sponsorship and reputation-building are crucially important influences on career-building in particular internal labour markets. In the medical profession, doctors have voiced their concerns about the processes of 'networking' and sponsorship which have excluded some of them from career progression in hospitals (registrar, surgeon and consultant positions). Both women and men have reported an 'old-boys' network' and the sponsoring of particular individuals, especially in surgery which is difficult, particularly for women, to break into. Other professions, such as law and the church, have similar networks of personal links and friendships to which it is extremely difficult for women to gain access.

In academic scientific careers, the process of reputation-building is particularly difficult for women. In the sociology of science, researchers have come up with some challenging ideas about how and why men are able to marginalize women, based on the management of scientific knowledge itself. These ideas can be extended to apply also to women and men in organizations. It has been argued in respect of the management, development and dissemination of scientific knowledge that core sets or small networks of male scientists involved in particular lines of research are responsible for legitimating new advances in knowledge in that line (Atkinson and Delamont, 1990). The position of women scientists is thereby rendered extremely difficult. Extending this to professional careers, Atkinson and Delamont have argued that core sets of (male) professionals are responsible for legitimating new knowledge and for disseminating information about professional competence and expertise. This is particularly the case in organizational careers. Most women are in lower-status professional and organizational positions or in the female enclaves of their occupations in internal labour markets. They are not visible, therefore, to core-set members. The processes of visibility and legitimacy, networking and sponsorship are important, therefore, in explaining some of the difficulties that women face in attempting to construct careers in the internal labour markets of professions and organizations.

Aspects of change in structural influences

The analysis of structural influences on careers has increased understanding and awareness of organizational and professional processes that constrain and limit the actions of women and men career-builders and reproduce gender segregation in occupations and organizations. The importance of ideological factors should also be emphasized, since organizational processes depend on a generalized acceptance of the 'reasonableness' of particular outcomes. The general acceptance of the beliefs that career success is individualistic, that promotion is merit-based, that certain jobs are most appropriately men's and others women's work and that women's family roles are more important anyway, continue to support and maintain the processes that have been considered. Such commonsense beliefs constitute the hegemonic ideology that shapes and differentially affects the promotional opportunities for women's and men's careers.

It is also necessary, however, for explanations to encompass structural change and its effects for women's and men's careers. Changes in this category include the economic, demographic and social contexts for careers. The economic conditions of prosperity and expansion or adversity and reduction are probably of paramount importance. There are also important organizational and professional changes. These might be general and applicable to all organizations, or specific to particular internal labour markets and sections of the professions.

Of great significance to the economy, for a short time, was the 'demographic timebomb' which was predicted to result in a shortage of young people in the labour market in the mid-1990s. As a result, organizations and professions were forced to pay more attention to the recruitment and retention of under-used groups. Women – particularly married women – were perceived to be such a group and employers such as banks and other service organizations, who had employed large numbers of women, looked to improve their provisioning of crèche and nursery facilities and opportunities for job-sharing and career breaks. The economic recession of the late 1980s and 1990s, however, together with rising unemployment, have reduced the need for employers to concern themselves with the retention of qualified but spare labour capacity. In the conditions of economic stringency of the 1990s, it has been suggested (Clement and MacIntyre, 1993) that commitments to equal opportunities initiatives for careers might be being abandoned. It is obvious, therefore, that structural constraints and opportunities for women's and men's careers are increased or reduced according to the supply-and-demand conditions in the economy for qualified and trained white-collar labour.

Another highly significant structural change has been the growth in part-time employment over the last two decades. According to Rubery, Horrell and Burchell (1994, p. 205) part-time work now accounts for over 23 per cent of the total stock of jobs in the economy. It is the fastest growing sector of employment: women's part-time jobs increased by 6.8 per cent between 1984 and 1987 (women's full-time jobs grew by 5.7 per cent and men's full-time jobs fell by more than 2 per cent). Rubery, Horrell and Burchell go on to argue, however, that part-time work is highly segregated and confined to feminized occupations in the service sector. They argue that there is no evidence, as yet, that it is becoming an alternative to full-time employment in all types of occupations.

The significance of this expansion in part-time employment for women's careers is difficult to determine categorically. Some researchers have argued that entry to part-time work leads to long-term disadvantage (Dex and Walters, 1989) since it results in extended periods in practitioner careers. It could, however, result in improvements in women's promotion achievements in the longer term, either if it speeds women's return to full-time employment or if a new pattern develops of part-time work or job-sharing going together with promotion in the career.

Fundamental structural changes are also occurring in organizations. Budgetary devolution, internal markets and market-testing all have important career implications for women and men in organizations. The extension of market principles of budgetary devolution as well as sub-contracting and short-term contracts, down-sizing and de-layering, are dramatically changing traditional career structures and ladders.

It is not yet clear whether such structural changes will constitute career constraints or opportunities for women and men in organizations. Some (e.g. Savage, 1992a; Cockburn, 1991) have challenged the supposed numerical improvements in women's career achievements in work organizations. Certainly the traditional, predictable life-time career has in many cases disappeared for women and men. Lower and middle levels of management have been cut back (Nicholson and West, 1988; Schofield, 1993). Self-employment and shorter-term contracts have increased, necessitating higher mobility as well as flexibility of skills and learning between posts and positions. This could well increase anxiety and insecurity for those (women and men) anticipating traditional careers, but promotion opportunities might increase for those individuals who are able and willing to change jobs and move positions. Career mobility has been a characteristic of men's rather than women's careers, but job changes, within a relatively small geographical area, *have* been a feature of women's working lives (Jenson, Hagen and Reddy, Eds, 1988). The pattern of women's job changes might well be adapted, therefore, to fit the new requirements (of flexibility, movement and change) for the working career. Structural influences have been and are powerful determinants of gender differences in careers. What historical research (e.g. Witz, 1992; Savage, 1992b) and contemporary comparative analysis (e.g. Dex and Shaw, 1986; Dex and Walters, 1989; Crompton and Le Feuvre, 1992) confirm is that career structures emerge as an outcome of conscious actions by key (male) actors in delineating male and female spheres of work opportunity in organizations and professions. Such delineations are then confirmed in commonsense (cultural) notions of what is appropriate and acceptable behaviour. Only by recognizing that male actions 'speak louder' in organizations can we explain why competitiveness, individualism, assertiveness and mobility are rewarded with career promotion, while cooperation, team-work, accommodation and loyalty are associated with practitioner careers. The experiences of the women and men scientists and engineers demonstrate some of these aspects of continuity in the gendering of careers but there are also important indications of variety in experiences as well as some changes in organizational processes.

Structural processes convincingly demonstrate the reproduction of institutional forms and even the adaptation of 'new' forms to accommodate change. Structural analysis is weakest in incorporating change, however. It tends to emphasize a fatalistic determinism by emphasizing the limits of change rather than the opportunities which might be perceived. A further limitation of structural explanations is the underestimation of the resistances of individual career-building actors themselves in such processes. The analysis of the reproduction of gender and organizational systems emphasizes determinants and thereby omits the untidy contradictions that are an increasing feature of actors' attempts to resist and challenge such processes in the workplace.

Action dimensions of careers

Cultural and structural influences on careers both focus primarily on the *determinants* of action, or at least the *constraints* on the career actions of women and men. When research focuses on experiences of career and data is collected on life- and career-histories, perhaps in in-depth interviews with professional women and men, then an alternative kind of explanatory model is likely to result. This is the 'subjective career' associated with interactionist research. Hughes (1937) identified a subjective dimension which consisted of individuals' own changing perspectives towards their careers: how workers actually experienced 'having a career'. In this case the concern is to shift the focus away from system and structural determinants towards the experiences of research subjects themselves. At the same time, however, the concept of the subjective career offered a means of linking individual experiences with organizational structures and cultural processes.

The extent to which qualified women and men *choose* a career provides a good example. Careers are not *determined* in any obvious way by cultural and structural factors and circumstances. Although cultural characteristics and structural processes influence and constrain choice, nevertheless to a certain extent individuals do choose between the opportunities available to them – assuming opportunities are available. Careers frequently result from earlier decisions which narrow the range of opportunities. Careers also result from happenstance, procrastination and serendipity and from chance encounters as well as from organizational changes and economic conditions.

Analysis of 'choice' in the subjective career is a complex phenomenon. The constraints, particularly for women, are real and powerful. Cultural notions of what is appropriately women's work (Beechey, 1987; Bates, 1990), as well as the requirement to combine paid and unpaid work responsibilities, work together to produce and reproduce gender-segregated occupations (horizontal segregation) as well as career and promotion differences (vertical segregation). Women are becoming better trained and qualified for careers (Banks *et al.*, 1992) and they have higher occupational aspirations (Crompton and Sanderson, 1990). But women's careers are still being constructed for the most part in gender-segregated occupations in organizations and professions. Under such constraints, a career 'choice' to pursue a practitioner career in a female-dominated profession constitutes a rational decision for women. The women in this study were developing careers in a 'non-traditional' profession, namely science and engineering in industry, although the men in the study were following gender-appropriate 'choices'.

The concepts of 'strategy' and 'identity' have been suggested as ways of emphasizing the actions, experiences and choices of women, as well as men themselves and of incorporating cultural and structural processes, as constraints that have to be managed, in the subjective career. The concepts of career strategy and identity are considered first; a consideration of changes in subjective career experiences follows.

Career strategies

The concept of strategy began and was first developed as an instrument of analysis in interactionist theoretical perspectives (Goffman, 1968, 1969). In the study of working careers, strategies are the ways in which individuals have (sometimes creatively) coped with, negotiated and managed cultural expectations as well as structural processes. In the analysis of women's career strategies, this has involved women's management of cultural role expectations, both personal and public, together with their negotiation of organizational career ladders and frameworks (Sheppard, 1989; Crompton and Le Feuvre, 1992). The strategies of women in particular occupations have been examined using methods such as life- and career-histories and auto/biographies. I have explored the strategies developed by women primary school headteachers

(Evetts, 1990) and women and men secondary school headteachers (Evetts, 1994b) in their management of personal responsibilities and careers in teaching. Using biographical accounts, Glazer and Slater (1987) analysed the strategies developed by individual women in medicine, psychiatric social work, university lecturing and social work, in their management of a male-defined model of career and career success.

The examination of the use of the concept of 'strategy' by Crow (1989), however, served to remind researchers that not all social actions are illuminated by interpretation as strategies. Two of Crow's points are of particular relevance to the analysis of the strategies in career development. First, can actions which are not long-term, rational, conscious and purposive usefully be conceived of as strategies? Second, can the actions of groups who are relatively powerless be interpreted as strategic without at the same time disguising and camouflaging the real sources of power? In the case of strategies for careers, an emphasis on the creativity of individuals in negotiating and managing constraints must not be allowed to obscure some of the resource differences which women and men have in constructing careers. Some men have both cultural as well as organizational advantages in developing strategies for their careers.

The concept of strategy enables researchers to explore the interrelationship between structure, culture and action by recognizing both the presence of cultural and structural constraints on careers and the active responses of social actors to such constraints. Career actions are no longer completely determined by social forces. Constraints are real but responses are variable. It is necessary to remember the potential difficulties, however, which might stem from describing the developments in women's careers as strategies. The imputation of rational, calculative, long-term planning, and of power resources to influence career outcomes, is probably inappropriate in the analysis of women's careers (Marshall, 1984).

Gender identities

An alternative concept to strategy as a way of focusing on experiences and linking experiences with cultural expectations and structural constraints, is the notion of identity. Whereas the idea of a career strategy implies an external goal and purpose outside of and separate from the individual and towards which the individual aims, the concept of career identity emphasizes an inner development and experience and a linking of self and structure. Whereas strategy implies conscious purpose, power and resources to affect an outcome, identity assumes neither but instead charts the interplay of self, actions, contexts and organizations. Identity has advantages in that it focuses on the unity of individual and structure (Abrams, 1982). Such a unity has often been emphasized. Strauss (1977, p. 764) stated that 'identities imply not merely personal histories but also social histories'.

In general, then, the concept of identity offers interesting possibilities for exploring the opportunities and constraints, the choices and contradictions for women and men in careered occupations. Such an approach enables opportunities and constraints to be examined simultaneously; the interconnections between them are assumed at the outset. The concept of career identity has been used to explore the routes into employment of young people who left school in the mid-1980s (Banks *et al.*, 1992). Identity has also been used in studies of unemployment and retirement where the central importance of work identity has been emphasized in perceptions of self and well-being (Breakwell, 1986). The concept of personal identity has been used by Marshall (1984) in her analysis of women managers: the ones she interviewed took a process approach to their careers, paying attention to satisfying their immediate personal needs rather than planning and looking ahead. These women found that further career opportunities tended to emerge unplanned when perceived as necessary.

The main difficulty with identity as an operational concept is the absence of an epistemology. Few researchers have considered the objectives, empirical specifications and requirements of such an approach. There are clear advantages to be gained, however, from using identity as an organizing concept for women's and men's careers. Gender and work identities will be fundamental in how individuals are placed and place themselves in the social system. The processes of identity formation and the procedures that result in the reproduction or the change of social structures are one and the same. The empirical study of 'becoming' has great potential for the development of our understanding about careers and gender differences in career perceptions.

Aspects of change in subjective careers

The experience of career for both women and men has been changing, though the changes for women have probably been greater. Women's increased participation in paid work, both full-time and particularly part-time, has been well-documented both in official statistics and in sociological analysis (Martin and Roberts, 1984; Firth-Cozens and West, Eds, 1991). When women and careers have been considered, the focus has tended to be on the constraints and difficulties that shape women's experiences. For the most part, women's careers, like their employment, are developed in gender-segregated occupational specialisms; and women's career achievements, whether measured in promotion, responsibility or salary terms, are less than their male colleagues.

Changes in women's subjective careers are significant, however, and are crucially linked to changes in structure and cultural processes. Changes in subjective careers include shifts in women's experiences, expectations and aspirations for their working lives and such changes are apparent. Changes can be illustrated in women's experience of career, as well as in the fields women are entering.

As more women achieve the qualifications for and experience of early promotion, they are less willing to give up their career positions in order to settle for unpaid work or practitioner or occupational positions. Crompton and Sanderson (1990) have noted how women are increasingly using the 'qualifications lever', as well as anti-discrimination legislation, in order to gain access to better paid, more responsible jobs and promotion positions. Women are also entering a wider range of professions and embarking on careers in institutions and organizations where gender differentiation was previously the norm. The church (Aldridge, 1994), the armed forces (Enloe, 1983) and engineering (McRae, Devine and Lakey, 1991) provide examples of women's infiltration into previously male-only careers. This study expands this line of development. Changes are slow, certainly, but aspects of change in both horizontal and vertical occupational segregation are nevertheless beginning to be demonstrated in women's career experiences.

Women as career actors can also create and develop new patterns and career alternatives, new ways of combining paid and unpaid work in their careers. Some women can (perhaps more easily than men) operationalize new styles of management (Tanton, Ed., 1994). Women are taking a lead in developing multifaceted (rather than unidimensional) careers (Evetts, 1994b). Other women are exploring the potential of self-employment and small-business proprietorship as a way of challenging the restrictions of the existing gender differences in the labour market (Rees, 1992).

There is evidence, then, that women's subjective careers, their career experiences and expectations are widening. The impetus behind such changes is probably increasing as the role-model effect impacts on subsequent generations. If the unusual subjective career experience becomes the norm, or even *a* norm, then changes in the structural and cultural influences on careers will also gain momentum.

There have been some, though different, changes in men's experience of career. Some men are experiencing disillusion with single-focus careers based *only* on promotion and achievement in the work organization (Scase and Goffee, 1989). Others are experiencing increased conflict in respect of partnership and family expectations and responsibilities (Thompson, Thomas and Maier, 1992), particularly in dual-career families. In addition, other changes in experience of career stem from organizational 'rationalizations' which have sometimes meant a reduction in promotion opportunities particularly at junior and middle levels of management in the organization. These changes have sometimes necessitated a drastic reappraisal of expectations for a traditional hierarchical career in the organization. Thus, for men in organizations, it is possible that structural changes are requiring and necessitating changes in career actions which might eventually bring about changes in career cultures.

Conclusion

This, then, is the model of continuity and change in the culture, structure and action dimensions of career that are used in this study. The careers of women and men scientists and engineers who work in industrial organizations are the subjects in this analysis. Further details of the respondents and the careers history research on which this study is based are provided in Chapter 3.

In conclusion to this chapter it is necessary to emphasize the interrelationship and mutually reinforcing effects of the three dimensions of career which have been described. The culture, structure and action dimensions of career work together and are inseparable, except in theoretical accounts and illustrations. Thus structure and culture arise out of actions and, at the same time, actions are influenced (perhaps determined) by structure and culture (Bourdieu and Wacquant, 1992). What people do in their careers always presupposes some kind of pre-existing structure (promotion ladders, rules of behaviour, cultural expectations and norms of behaviour) but in what they do, people simultaneously recreate the structure and culture anew or alternatively new structures emerge and are developed. The processes of structuration (Giddens, 1984), and the possibilities of reproduction or change through the creation of new structures, need to be kept constantly in mind.

For the most part it is through externally and internally generated change that altered career expectations and actions can bring about changes in organizational career structures and cultures. Alternatively, changes in organizational career structures can necessitate alterations in career actions and expectations which might eventually modify career cultures. Career experiences and actions and career structures and cultures have an internal dynamic and a mutual interdependence. Experiences of career are part of the same mutually reinforcing process whereby actions and structures both interact and reinforce a career outcome. Conditions of change form the best contexts in which to observe the interrelation of structural, cultural and action dimensions of career.

This model of career is applied and elaborated in subsequent chapters as the careers history accounts of the women and men scientists and engineers unfold and are used to explore the dynamics of careers in organizations. First, it is necessary to focus on the concepts and categories of 'scientist' and 'engineer' and to consider the theoretical issues to do with class, profession and organization which have occupied researchers interested in these categories of professional workers. This review of conceptual issues is undertaken in Chapter 2. In Chapter 3, the careers history respondents, who have provided the data used in this study, are introduced and the epistemology used in the analysis is explained.

Chapter 2

Theoretical Issues: Class, Profession and Organization

Any examination of stability and change in the professions of science and engineering, and of the culture, structure and action dimensions of stability and change, needs to begin by reviewing the theoretical traditions within each jurisdiction. What questions have social scientists asked about scientists and what issues have been addressed in respect of engineers? What are the problematics about scientific and technological labour for sociologists? What explanations have been offered for their market position and social place in contemporary social systems? It seems to be generally agreed that national context, rather than technological development, industrial structure or class relations, offers the best explanation of the social position of scientific and technological labour. Smith (1990, p. 456) has argued in respect of research on engineers that 'we begin and end in national history or culturalism' even when researchers consider the structural determinants of how such workers are formed, used and organized.

In his summary of the key debates in respect of engineers, Smith (1990, p. 452) listed the following: 'the growth and social function of technical workers in the capitalist division of labour; their role in the future structure of the economy as it allegedly shifts towards so-called "knowledge" industries; the question of the class position of engineers and how class and nation interact; the role of engineers in management and economic success; and, finally, the politics of professional representation'. In respect of research on scientists, Atkinson and Delamont (1990, p. 92) identified three kinds of research focus: programmatic statements about scientists and their place in society; empirical research among established practitioners; and research on socialization into the occupation. To this list should be added debates about the nature of the scientific community as well as of scientific knowledge itself. There has, then, been some overlap in the concerns of researchers interested in science and engineering jurisdictions. There have also been some differences in focus. Thus, for engineers their occupational context has been perceived as industrial and organizational capitalism while for scientists their occupational context has been perceived as fellow scientists or the scientific community. This is a somewhat false distinction, however, since, with the exception of academic scientists, the large majority of scientists will also be working in industrial organizational contexts.

When the objective is to understand the processes of career in science and engineering occupations in industrial organizations, however, and any gender differences in career patterns and experiences, then consideration of the relevant theoretical issues has to be wider and more general. As the previous chapter showed, there is a need to include culture, structure and action influences on career aspirations as well as career outcomes. It is also essential to include interactionist perspectives more generally, in order to begin to understand some of the gender differences in career experiences. It is proposed here to review the debates on class, professions and organizations, as these relate to the career processes of scientists and engineers working in industry. The processes of class, profession and organization are closely interrelated and mutually reinforcing, in the experiences of career. The issue of gender can also be discussed in all three contexts. This is followed by a brief review of professional competitions in organizations and the expanding influence of international regulation on careers in professional fields.

Class

The scientists and engineers to be considered here are salaried professionals. Some are managers or aspirant managers; they are part of a middle-class. They work in industrial organizations; they are 'employees with autonomy, authority, career expectations, a monthly salary, fringe benefits, and a certain security' (Whalley, 1986, p. 185). Professional scientists and engineers working in industry are part of 'trusted labour' or the 'service class' (Goldthorpe, 1982).

The application of this Weberian or market-based definition of class, where the class structure is differentiated according to possession of marketable skills and resources, has been criticized in its application to engineers by Smith (1990). His comments can also be applied to organizational scientists. He claimed that the conditions that define the service class can be appropriated by manual workers either through struggle or through management decision; thus distinctions thought to be exclusive can become inclusive over time. He also argued that differentiation within the staff-worker category, particularly perhaps between the career/promotion successful and others, was obscured by the all-embracing notion of a 'service class'. Such an all-inclusive concept could be perceived as unhelpful, therefore, in understanding the culture, structure and action influences on careers, in that it minimized important status, authority and power dimensions within the service class.

When Smith goes on to review class identification, he argues that this is critically dependent on national contexts and historical antecedents. In Britain the line between professional engineer/scientist and craft/technical/production worker has always been difficult to draw – and all grades of worker have used the titles 'engineer' and 'scientist'. Employers have not (until recently) sought to divide such workers according to educational qualifications and have facilitated movement by encouraging technical workers to acquire certificates and diplomas (Whalley, 1986). In Britain, therefore, technical workers such as professional scientists and engineers have been perceived as 'workers', though as staff or white-collared sections of workers. Again, the career and promotion position of the engineers and scientists is critical, since promotion into management significantly differentiates workers within the staff category.

In other countries in Europe and elsewhere, the situation is different and the professional titles and licences to practise are confined to those with the required diplomas. In France, graduate technical labour is straightforwardly incorporated into supervisory responsibilities and a new class of technical managers (*les cadres*) is developing a distinctive sociopolitical identity (Boltanski, 1987). In America, universities provide industry with already seg-regated technical labour and a close association with managerial careers (Zussman, 1985). Their class and professional identities are easier to desig-nate, therefore, although again career and promotion progress are probably significant distinguishing and differentiating factors.

More recently, researchers on class have been developing ideas on life-style and consumption as indicators of class identity and class influence (Crompton, 1993). The work of Bourdieu (1986, 1987) has been significant in this shift of emphasis. For Bourdieu, class is to do with social relations in general and how it affects the conditions of existence, dispositions, condition-ing and endowments of power and capital (Brubaker, 1985). Bourdieu ident-ifies four 'forms of capital': economic, cultural, social and symbolic. Possession of these different forms differentially empowers individuals who thereby come to share a similar 'habitus'. Bourdieu defined 'habitus' as 'a system of dispo-sitions shared by all individuals who are products of the same conditionings' (1987, p. 762).

Bourdieu developed the concept of 'habitus' in class analysis and it has been used particularly by researchers interested in the new middle class (Crompton, 1993). It was important to differentiate the habitus of different sections of the old and new middle class. It was also necessary to link habitus with lifestyles and consumption patterns and to explore how these related to differences in career expectations, experiences and achievements. Such con-cerns renewed interest in the aspects of change and stability in class formation and development, as well as focusing attention on the structure and action dimensions of class processes.

The concept of habitus has also been used to examine some of the aspects of professional power and influence. Atkinson (1983) used the term 'indeter-minate' knowledge in his analysis of professional socialization. The essential performance skills of a profession are never explicitly taught, but are believed to be personal, natural and even innate. Those who undergo lengthy training and socialization in professional training schools can assimilate the oral tra-ditions and technical skills of a profession. But essential practitioner knowledge, particularly that associated with success and high achievement, remains indeterminate, never clarified, codified, explained or taught. Atkinson sees the preservation of the exclusiveness of such indeterminate knowledge as essential for professionals' power, status and authority. Atkinson and Delamont (1990) have used both indeterminacy and habitus in their explanation of the marginal position of women in the professions and in professional science. Women are able to acquire the technical skills required by a profession, but not the habitus. It is the very indeterminacy of the habitus which makes it unaccessible. Women's marginal status is due to 'their perceived failure to behave in ways which reveal their mastery of the indeterminate: that is, their failure to share the habitus' (1990, p. 107).

When the concept of gender is linked with that of (middle) class, then different kinds of explanation are produced for class formation and change, as well as for class identity and consciousness, class consequences and effects. The concept of career and of gender differences in career has been useful in this kind of analysis. It has long been acknowledged that career progress in the middle classes has traditionally been achieved by couples operationalizing two-person single-career strategies (Evetts, 1993). In this model, the wife supports the career progress and development of the husband either by being a full-time home-maker and carer or by combining home-making with an occupation that does not entail career commitment (Finch, 1983). It was not until later, however, and with the use of historical data, that gender differences were demonstrated in the workplace itself. Researchers began to show how gender segregation within occupations and professions enabled men to progress in their careers while women continued to do the backstage work. Savage (1992b) has demonstrated this in banking between 1880 and 1940. Witz (1992) charts the emergence of the division of labour within the medical profession in the late-nineteenth and early-twentieth centuries. Savage (1992a) has argued that, rather than distinguishing class from gender, it is necessary to indicate the close connection between gender and middle-class formation and development.

Some of the issues raised in this kind of research are also pertinent in science careers in the analysis of gender and career in science and engineering. Women have been recruited to do different kinds of work to men. They have tended to develop practitioner careers, doing the detailed laboratory work and developing careers as research assistants, rather than taking part in policy decisions and building scientific reputations (King, 1994). Until recently, very few women had even entered engineering careers and their tiny minority position has rendered them more visible and more vulnerable (Kanter, 1977) in career terms. The work women have done in their scientific and engineering careers has also enabled men to progress into managerial careers while the women have continued to do the backstage work. There is then an emergent division of labour within these professions which mirrors that in other professions and is more generally part of the process of middle-class formation and development.

Profession

In sociological analysis of the professions, the early research focus was the characteristics or traits of professions which made them distinctive occupational groups (Jackson, Ed., 1970). In the 1970s the sociology of professions shifted its emphasis on to power and interests and the monopoly control over markets for professional services which the professions enjoyed (Johnson, 1972; Dingwall and Lewis, Eds, 1983). A later concern was Abbott's *system* of professions (1988) which emphasized the interrelations and competitions between (and within) professions over jurisdictional boundaries and control of work. Abbott's work is discussed in the final section of this chapter. For the professional scientists and engineers that are discussed here, competition within the industrial organization was a feature of their experience. This *could* be perceived as competition over jurisdiction or work boundaries, but more important in the organizational context was competition over career and promotion.

Other debates within the profession's literature are also pertinent to the present discussion. The large majority of professional engineers and most scientists (with the exception of engineering consultants and some research scientists) are salaried employees working in large- or small-scale industrial or service organizations. This used to be considered a negative factor which differentiated corporate scientists and engineers from other professionals who were perceived as largely self-employed and exercising autonomy and independence in their relations with clients. This constituted one of the myths of professionalism, however, since the majority in almost all professions are now salaried employees in service or industrial organizations. For a while, in the sociology of the professions, this reduction of autonomy was considered as 'the proletarianization of the professions', as the standardization of work practices in organizations was seen to reduce the discretion and independence of professionals (McKinlay 1982; McKinlay and Arches, 1985).

Attempts to introduce the assessment and appraisal of professionals have been interpreted in similar ways (Lawn and Ozga, 1981; Lawn and Grace, Eds, 1987). But this argument, in both its strong and weak form, was effectively countered by Murphy (1990). Murphy argued that there *has* been increased specialization of professionals, and that professionals working in organizations *have* lost control over the goals and purposes to which their work is put. This did not constitute proletarianization, however. Rather it consisted of the *bureaucratization* of professionals. Corporate science and engineering provide clear examples of the important distinction between proletarianization and bureaucratization. Professional scientists and engineers working in industrial organizations have not lost control of the knowledge, the technical job decisions and the process of work. However, they have rarely had control over the products produced or the aims of the organization. There are organizational management systems which control science and engineering professionals but their technical autonomy is not threatened.

Two other conditions identified by Murphy (1990) also need consideration in respect of the professions of science and engineering in industrial organizations. The first was developments in micro-electronics and computers which, it has been claimed, have provided management with the technological means to control the work of professionals. In respect of engineering, engineers are the professionals who are developing and providing this new technology. However, they are not controlling its application and use and are, like other professionals, controlled in their own work practices by its application (e.g. computer-assisted design, testing and specifications).

The second condition Murphy described was where professionals are increasingly managed by managers trained in management schools, whereas they had been used to being managed by their fellow professionals who were sympathetic to their needs and interests. Competition over career within industrial organizations is an important feature of the experiences of scientists and engineers. In industry these professionals, for the most part, are still managed by fellow senior science and engineering professionals. Certainly in middle and even senior management, professional scientists and engineers are well-represented in the management of science, technological and technical work in industrial organizations. At the very highest levels, however, at director and main board director level, science and engineering managers are in career competition with accountants and economists, bankers, industrialists, academics and even politicians, over control of the goals and aims of the organization itself. This kind of competition, within the industrial organization and in respect of career and promotion, seems the most relevant application of Abbott's (1988) system model to the careers of the scientists and engineers in this study. The last section of this chapter returns to this discussion.

When gender is incorporated into theoretical models of professional processes, competition over jurisdiction is perceived in a different way and competition over career is gender differentiated. Researchers on women professionals have described the competitive jurisdictional processes of internal demarcation of professional work, of the ghetto-ization of women and of the subordination of female areas of competence. These processes have been operationalized by cultural as well as structural means, and have been described in Chapter 1 (pp. 8–19).

The concepts of the professional closure, internal differentiation and subordination of female professional areas and competencies have all been explored and illustrated in particular professions. Thus, for example, Witz (1992) described various strategies of social closure (exclusionary, inclusionary, demarcationary and dual closure) within the medical profession in the nineteenth and twentieth centuries. Medical professionalization in the nineteenth century is widely acknowledged to be the paradigmatic case of exclusionary closure which used both credentialist and legalistic tactics. Aspiring medical women replied with inclusionary closure which was essentially a usurpationary struggle. The paradigmatic case of demarcationary closure was the troubled inter-occupational relations between medical men and midwives in the latter half of the nineteenth century. Midwives replied with a dual-closure strategy which contained both usurpationary and exclusionary dimensions. Nurses similarly engaged in a dual-closure strategy in attempts to achieve nurse registration, self-government and control of training. But the nurses' professional project was never realized in closure terms since medical dominance continued to be the overriding factor. Then, in the analysis of gender and radiography, Witz introduced the concept of internal demarcation as a sub-type of exclusionary closure. In this case, male radiographers worked to internally demarcate between male (technical skills) and female (patient-centred skills) spheres of competence within radiography and to devalue the female.

Similar processes of closure, internal demarcation and subordination of the female areas of expertise have been described in other professions. Teaching is widely recognized as a gender differentiated (horizontally and vertically) profession (Acker, 1989). Social work is similarly becoming increasingly gender differentiated as promotion, managerial and policy-making aspects become a male preserve while female social workers continue the practice with clients. The practice of law is gender-differentiated, with women confined to family jurisdictions while men predominate in the high-status and career-preparatory areas of criminal and finance law. In science, such gender processes have been described (Cole, 1979), though there has been less study of organizational scientists. Similarly in engineering, the gender processes of professional closure, internal demarcation and subordination of the female within the industrial organization await further study. In general, most of the detailed theoretical analysis on gender and career has been done within the context of organizations and bureaucracies rather than in the context of the professions; this work is considered next.

Organization

The classic theoretical framework for understanding organizations and bureaucracy was established by Weber (1948, 1968). The resultant ideal-type models of organizational structure and functioning suggested inherent progress towards reason and rationality, although Weber was well aware of the disadvantages of bureaucratic modes of social organization. Recent writers have developed and refined the original ideal-type models and have drawn important links between organization and class theory. Thus Goldthorpe (1982, p. 170) described the service class as dependent on the 'processes of bureaucratic appointment and achievement'. Others such as Lash and Urry (1987) and Crompton and Le Feuvre (1992) have seen considerable explanatory potential in the concept of an organizational or bureaucratic *career*. Lash and Urry see the development of a career as central to the identification of the service class. In the service class, individuals are bound to their organizations by loyalty in exchange for a career (Goldthorpe, 1982; Abercrombie and Urry, 1983; Lash and Urry, 1987, quoted in Crompton and Le Feuvre, 1992, p. 106).

The classic bureaucracy and organization are, however, dependent on a particular configuration of gender relations. Savage and Witz (Eds, 1992) have reviewed the importance of gender in the development of modern bureaucracies. Thus bureaucratic officials have to be free of domestic and personal responsibilities in order to fulfil their professional duties and achieve their career potential. Service-class promotion is dependent on the non-service-class work of women, both in the work organization and in the home (Crompton, 1986). The bargain struck between individuals and organizations, where loyalty is exchanged for promotion and career, is crucially dependent on a gendered division of labour. The reproduction as well as the adaptation of the bureaucratic organization, the bureaucratic career and the service class itself is shaped and formed by the gender paradigm.

Other researchers have emphasized the cultural underpinnings of organizational structures. Hearn *et al.* (1989) explored the pervasiveness of sexuality in organizations and the interrelations of sexuality and power in the reproduction of organizational life. Pringle (1989) focused on discourses of power rather than organizational processes. Using comparative material, Crompton and Le Feuvre (1992) highlight the difficulties faced by women managers in the finance sector in the UK and France. The employment patterns of French women are similar to those of French men. In Britain the patterns are different, with British women experiencing broken employment and part-time work. Yet at the level of the organization, the experiences of French and British women are similar. They face common problems when trying to progress along organizational career routes and paths designed for and dominated by men. These similarities and differences in experience can be used to argue that processes within organizations themselves, rather than within families, are probably the most crucially important influences on women's careers.

Savage (1992a) has also argued that understanding organizations holds the key to understanding the wider social processes of class formation, change and reproduction. In order to understand the significance of the expansion of the female professional workforce, it is essential to relate that issue to class formation and to the role of organizations and career hierarchies in middle-class development and change. Savage shows how despite the increase of women in positions of expertise (in banking), remarkably few hold positions of real power in their banking organizations. It is necessary to recognize the significance of organizations in gender inequality and in class reproduction and change. He goes on to analyse the differential gender usage of class assets (the property, organization and skill assets analysed by Wright, 1985). Skill assets are less intrinsically gendered; successful women and men both use skills assets. But whereas women are dependent on skill assets, men are not. Men also use organizational assets since organizational hierarchies are important vehicles of male power. When women use their skills assets in their careers, they become professional specialists but their specialization then renders them ill-equipped and ill-experienced for positions of power and authority in the organization. In these ways, organizations have changed to incorporate women professionals but organizational power is retained for men.

Organizational research has therefore shifted the focus away from demonstrating the barriers for women (which was characteristic of the research on the professions) to showing how in organizations gender differences are actively constructed, adapted and reproduced. Crompton (1993) has called this a postmodernist shift in social thought since models now have to incorporate cultural as well as structural productions and to include diversity and variety of experience alongside generalized conceptions of stability and change. In general, it seems that gender-employment patterns, expectations and experiences do change and there is considerable variation in experiences, but 'a formal equality of access is not adequate to achieve a real equality of practice' (Crompton and Le Feuvre, 1992, p. 115). Bureaucracy and organizations result in different outcomes for men's and women's careers, even when the men and women are in equivalent jobs. Nevertheless, there is considerable variation among women and men. Women can develop bureaucratic careers and some do; some, but not all, remain childfree, calculate promotion moves and progress up linear career hierarchies. Even for women such as these, however, their gender remains critical. They become *women* managers rather than managers and the difference is still emphasized. Cultural modes of production reinforce organizational structures and, at the same time, generate diversities in experience which might ultimately result in organizational change.

Professional competitions and international regulations

From the brief review of theoretical developments in class, professions and organization, it is necessary to move on to outline the wider contexts in which corporate science and engineering careers are constructed and developed. These contexts consist of the macro-level processes of competition that operate between and within professional and industrial organizations, as well as at nation-state and international levels. Such processes influence the opportunities available to individual experiences of career as well as the limitations which constrain them.

Abbott referred to these bodies of expertise as professional jurisdictions; and professionals aim to control their expert knowledge systems in their applied as well as in their academic forms. Abbott defined 'jurisdiction' as the link between a profession and its work (1988, p. 20) and he considered this to be the central phenomenon of professional life. Jurisdictions were created in work and anchored by formal and informal structures. There was both a culture and a structure of professional jurisdiction.

Abbott argued further that jurisdictional boundaries are perpetually in dispute. Control of knowledge and its application is constantly being challenged as others attack that control and try to gain access to existing jurisdictions or to create new ones. He claimed that interprofessional competition over jurisdictions was a fundamental fact of professional life; that new professions develop when new jurisdictions develop or old jurisdictions become vacant. Hence there is a need for a *system* model of professions which emphasizes their interrelations, their competitions and their control of bodies of knowledge and its applications. 'It is control of work that brings the professions into conflict with each other and makes their histories interdependent' (Abbott 1988, p. 19). It is contended here, however, that it is not only control of work that brings the professions into conflict with each other but also competition over career. Career competition is another aspect of professional conflict which is particularly prevalent in careers constructed in organizations.

These two aspects of professional competition are considered separately. Then a new dimension of professional competition is considered. This consists of the expanding area of the international regulation of professions and professional services and of associated mechanisms of deregulation in national contexts.

Jurisdictional competition

The workplace is the main arena (rather than the alternatives, the legal system, public opinion and the State, all of which were described by Abbott) in which the claims over control of the work of corporate professional scientists and engineers have been made. Within the organization, the interprofessional division of labour which operates in an open market is replaced by an intra-organizational division of tasks and responsibilities. Abbott has argued (1988, p. 65) that there might be formal job descriptions and contracts which recognize professional boundaries. The reality of everyday work cultures and work experiences is rather different, however. Actual divisions of tasks in offices, laboratories and on shop floors are established through custom and negotiation and they hold only for short periods of time. As work loads increase, jurisdictional boundaries are likely to be ignored as pressure is on professionals as well as technicians to get results and to complete tasks. In times of labour shortage, professional posts might be filled by untrained staff. Alternatively, in times of labour plenty, technical positions might be filled by professionally trained staff. Professionals operationalize craft techniques, as when a professional scientist or engineer carries out a test procedure or repairs a machine usually looked after by a technician. Rigid demarcation lines are hard to maintain, therefore, particularly in overworked worksites. Abbott argued that a form of knowledge transfer he called 'workplace assimilation' would result. In Abbott's description, non-professionals learn a craft version of the professions' knowledge. Alternatively, professionals carry out craft procedures. Thus, in the industrial workplace the potential for competition over professional jurisdictions is increased.

These workplace challenges to professional jurisdictions have been supported recently by educational changes in Britain and the creation of a new National Council for Vocational Qualifications (NCVQ) system of certification. The NCVQ framework has important implications for all professional groups. It provides a set of alternative qualifications which will be available at the level of, and in competition with, professional qualifications. NVQ is decided on the basis of competencies and of those so far decided, civil engineers (graduates) are in the framework at level 4. The important point here, and the reason NVQs pose a challenge to professional engineers, as to other professions, is that employers can now legally use non-professionally trained staff to do tasks traditionally reserved for those with professional qualifications, provided competence can be shown.

In addition to competition over professional and non-professional boundaries, there are other forms of professional competition. There are intraprofessional rivalries within the organization, as the fields of science and engineering are made up of a number of different specialisms. Scientists have a specialized professional knowledge and identity and will be recruited by the organization as 'chemists', 'biologists', etc. Engineers also compete largely by speciality (mechanical, electrical, materials) and could be treated as several different professions. Within the work organization, there is a question over the extent to which scientists and engineers are interchangeably competent. Job descriptions might specify a particular type of scientist or engineer but in laboratories, factories and offices, scientists and engineers might be called on to move beyond a narrow specialist expertise. Similarly, production problems do not necessarily fall into neat academic categories. In team projects of different specialists there is likely to be competition, as well as cooperation, in report-findings, conclusions and recommendations.

A final area of competition is from new professional jurisdictions. According to Abbott (1988), new professions develop when jurisdictions are vacant. This might happen because they constitute new knowledge areas and new applications, or because an earlier professional occupant no longer controls the work. A vacancy frequently occurs when knowledge and expertise in an area expand such that a new specialism develops. This might start with the development of internal, intraprofessional differences which subsequently develop into new professional jurisdictions.

The professions of science and engineering are highly susceptible to new research findings and developments and to changes in the character of their central tasks and procedures as new research and new applications are incorporated in industrial production (and old ones decline). The development of internal differences and specialisms is directly linked to the development of new jurisdictions and new professionalisms. Thus, for example, communications engineering is still a rapidly fragmenting specialist area with the continuing development of new superconductive materials and their application. Similarly, robotics and biological engineering represent areas of growing internal difference, specialism and new professional jurisdiction. Finally, computer-assisted design (CAD) constitutes a new area of professional competition which will affect all engineering jurisdictions.

Career competition

It could be argued that most of the jurisdictional competitions outlined above are, in fact, competitions over career. Jurisdictional competition over control of work in the workplace, or over control of new developments, or professional rivalries within the organization, can be perceived as competitions about promotion, increased authority, status and income in the organization. Such an interpretation also leads to the identification of other forms of professional rivalry and competition.

Every profession has a range of typical careers. Because of the organizational location of the scientists and engineers in this study, their careers are mainly limited to those available within the organization itself. The two most common career routes are either into a professional specialism or into management within the organization. A third but much less common alternative is a career move out of the organization into independent, freelance consultancy work or into a different career such as teaching.

The first career route in the organization, into a professional specialism, involves a narrowing of focus on to a technical specialist task, problem or operation. Such a career involves doing research and development, writing papers and attending conferences, perhaps even jointly supervising research students in partnership with a university department. The research would generally involve the *application* of knowledge, bearing in mind the organizational context, but fruitful research partnerships between academics and professional specialists are often formed. Within the organization itself, such a career route might end if a particular line of development did not prove to be economically viable. A change to another specialism would then be required. Where a particular line of research proved to be operational and economic, a move out of the organization into self-employment, consultancy or the development of a new enterprise might constitute a possible career opportunity.

The most common career route in the past, however, for scientists and engineers in organizations involved a move into management. Promotion in science and engineering careers in organizations usually required a move away from doing the scientific and engineering work to managing others who were doing it. This career route into management compounded the problem of professional identity for engineers (Finniston, 1980) as well as for scientists. It also resulted in another long-standing form of professional competition between scientists/engineers and managers in the organization.

The growth of business management qualifications (MBAs) has fuelled this competition. Individuals with MBA qualifications are beginning to gain control of the person-management work in industrial organizations. Some are also former scientists or engineers and are therefore sympathetic to scientific and technological interests. Others are not, however, and are armed only with the academic knowledge systems and applications of management theory itself. This constitutes real career competition for professional scientists and engineers over control of management work in the organization.

Recent changes in both industrial and service organizations have resulted in a general reduction in person-management work and an increase in expertise management. Savage (1992b) has demonstrated how organizational changes in banking have increased the number of positions with the title 'manager' but how most of these posts only involve managing a task and not other workers. I have confirmed similar changes in my own research on two large industrial organizations (Evetts, 1994c). It seems, therefore, that a reduction in people-management posts in organizations, together with an expansion of specialized professional management qualifications, constitute a new dimension of professional competition over career between scientists, engineers and others in organizations.

International regulation

The period since the end of the Second World War has seen an increase in transnational regulations and international agreements affecting professionals and their services. This internationalization of professional regulation constitutes a series of new challenges and competitions for professional jurisdictions. For professional scientists and engineers, these new battles are occurring outside the workplace and beyond the organization. Claims now have to be pursued in the legal arena and in the contexts of international relations.

Science and engineering, in terms of their expertise and applications, have been international, probably since their first links with industry. This century, however, has witnessed the increased globalization of capital as multinational corporations throughout the world have expanded trade and production into new markets. Scientists and particularly engineers working for such multinationals have been mobile, alongside their organizations' capital. Scientists and engineers have had to comply with different national regulations as well as with their company's requirements. This has resulted in a growing recognition of the need for international agreements in respect of products and equipment, professional practice and services as well as requirements in respect of the environment, health and safety.

The European Union (EU) made professional education an early priority. Most professions are now covered by regulations that define a common basis of competence for licensing. These regulations allow EU nationals to move freely throughout the Community, subject, in theory, only to such language-skills testing as may be locally required. In practice there continue to be disputes. Some British engineering qualifications have a limited acceptability in European countries which have traditionally afforded the profession a higher status and a longer education and training period. The First General

Systems Directive ensured the *recognition* of professional engineering qualifications, but such qualifications are not regarded as *equivalent* by Member States for practice and employment purposes.

The objective of international recognition of qualifications has never been confined to Europe, however: other international agreements (e.g. between former commonwealth or NATO countries) have proceeded prior to or alongside the development of EU directives. The increased mobility of scientists and engineers across national boundaries is not yet an established trend beyond the already existing mobility that stems from the growing internationalization of production. In respect of competition over professional careers, however, the movement of scientists and engineers to higher-paying jobs and countries must be anticipated. The increased mobility of academic scientists has already been documented. Similarly, a movement of trainee scientists and engineers to lower-cost, shorter-duration education and training centres might be expected. Increased competition over jurisdictions and careers is a distinct possibility.

It is also possible that more challenges to professional closure are likely to occur. Moves to deregulate professional activity in order to widen access is not just a UK phenomenon. Partly as a result of EU directives, but also as a result of globalization pressures generally, the professions are being forced to adopt a role as service providers in an increasingly crowded and competitive market – competitive not just on price but, more importantly, on the range of services offered. For professional scientists and engineers, the challenges from semi-professionals offering a wider range of expertise and experience are likely to increase. Continuing control of science and engineering jurisdictions and careers, even in the comparative safety of industrial organizations, cannot be assumed.

In the internationalization processes that have been considered, legal instruments are the new currencies by which agreements are reached. Regulations, directives, soft laws and private agreements are the legal tools of internationalization. The intrusion of law into all professional jurisdictions constitutes an additional professional competition. In science and engineering, a new jurisdictional field of scientific and engineering law might constitute the latest market gap. In order to enter this arena, scientists and engineers would have to leave the comparative safety of their organizations and compete with legal professionals in the international field. Some moves have already been made as the growth of professional patent agents testifies. It seems that the control of professional scientific and engineering work will increasingly take place in legal fields and in international legal arenas. Increased competition in respect of scientific and engineering careers could also be played out in international arenas as well as in organizational ones.

This brief review of theoretical issues highlights the particular and distinctive position of the corporate professional scientists and engineers that are the concern of this book. The class, professional and organizational contexts for their careers have been described and the processes and competitions that operate at organizational, professional and increasingly at international levels have been outlined.

These scientists and engineers are professionals, yet they are employees of complex industrial organizations. They are clearly middle- or service-class in terms of their educational capital and salary status, but their possession of other forms of capital is diverse and highly variable. Their position within the service class is critically determined by their career and promotion achievements in the organization and by their ability to take on management forms of knowledge and expertise – and hence to neglect their professional scientific or engineering identities. Their habitus is unclear since, unlike their colleagues in academic science and engineering, their networks are industrial and organizational rather than professionally orientated.

It is also necessary to incorporate the wider influences on career which include the intra- and interprofessional competitions over jurisdictions. Professional interdependence and rivalries over control of work and promotion in the career are operationalized within organizations, but are increasingly being played out in international legal arenas. International agencies and professions are working to modify national regulatory and licensing systems for practitioners, to change education and training arrangements allowing increased access to professional positions and sometimes to alter spheres of professional work.

Alongside and interrelated with these complexities and contradictions, the scientists and engineers have a gender identity. Their gender, together with their personal responsibilities and relationships, will need to be incorporated in this examination of their career experiences and outcomes. For years, the public and private dimensions of career were separated. This resulted in an incomplete, indeed inaccurate, understanding of the processes of class, profession and organization. Such a model was never adequate to understand the interrelations between the structure, culture and action dimensions of career and change as well as of stability in career processes.

Chapter 3

The Careers History Study: Methods, Respondents and Organizations

Chapter 1 identified a number of different types of research model for studying careers and analysing gender differences in them. The point was made there that different research methodologies, asking different sorts of question and producing different sorts of data, are likely to generate different kinds of explanation for the interrelation of gender and career in organizations. This chapter explains the methodology and the epistemology used in the careers history research project in this study and gives the background details about the respondents and their work organizations.

This study incorporates careers history data from 41 respondents, 21 scientists and 20 engineers. The categories 'scientist' and 'engineer' are used to describe the routes and positions through which individual respondents developed their careers. The terms do not necessarily reflect respondents' current posts, however, since several would now be more appropriately labelled as project or system managers. The scientist category also included five respondents (three women, two men) who had developed careers in computing and programming systems. In the analysis, these five respondents are differentiated from the other scientists whenever their experiences warranted separation. These scientists (programmers) and engineers, 31 women and 10 men, worked for two large industrial organizations. One was a high-technology engineering company for which the pseudonym 'Airmax' is used (15 women engineers, 5 men). The other was a company manufacturing a diverse range of consumer products and employing large numbers of professional scientists and programmers for which the pseudonym 'Marlands' is used (16 women scientists, 5 men). The careers history group were all graduates or equivalent and their careers were developing in the two organizations.

This research followed the successful use of similar careers history data in other projects, on primary school headteachers (Evetts, 1990) and on secondary school headteachers (Evetts, 1994b). A great deal had been learned from these projects about careers in a public service like education, about the career determinants of and the career choices available to the profession of teachers in British schools. It also became increasingly clear that professionals work in the way they do not just because of the skills they have or have not learned in their training and experience. The ways professionals operate are also grounded in how their organizations work and in their individual backgrounds and biographies. Their career histories – their opportunities and aspirations, their achievements and disappointments, their ideals and disillusionments, their overall experiences – are all vitally important for their professional identities. Relationships with their colleagues are also highly significant for their commitment, enthusiasm and morale. So too are their private relationships and their domestic and personal responsibilities. All these things affect the quality of the professional work that is accomplished.

From headteachers' careers, the move was made to the careers of women and men professional scientists and engineers working in industrial organizations. This constituted a very different environment for careers and career-building. The objective, however, was the same. Through detailed and intensive investigation of individual experiences, the aim was to demonstrate what the lives and careers of professional scientists and engineers working in industrial organizations are like, how they differ along gender lines and how they are being re-shaped by organizational changes. The aim was also to show the connections between formal careers and private lives and how each is embedded in the other.

The subjective career

Some of the themes to do with research on the subjective career were explained in Chapter 1 (pp. 19–23). The distinction between objective and subjective dimensions of career was suggested by Hughes (1937), who contrasted the formal structure of posts, statuses and positions of the 'career ladder' (objective dimension) with individuals' own changing perspectives towards their careers – how they actually experienced having a career. Hughes described the subjective career as 'the moving perspective in which the person sees his life as a whole and interprets the meaning of his various attributes, actions and the things which happen to him' (Hughes, 1958, p. 409).

In the analysis of subjective careers, there is no prior assumption of promotion and progress, nor do job changes have to be regular, systematic or strategic. This has particular relevance to the study of women's careers but it is not exclusive to women. Nor does the subjective career have to be centred solely on developments in the work sphere. The subjective career is a process: change, adjustment and adaptation are implicit. 'The adult career is usually the product of a dialectical relationship between self and circumstances. As the result of meeting new circumstances, certain interests may be reformulated, certain aspects of the self changed or crystallized, and, in consequence, new directions envisaged' (Sikes, Measor and Woods, 1985, p. 2). In the subjective career, 'career contingencies' (usually events in the personal or private sphere which affect a career) can become a major part of 'having a career', if that is how the individual perceives them.

When researchers study subjective careers, the focus is on individuals' experiences. As a result, careers are shown to be diverse, complex and highly variable, not necessarily confined to a smooth unilinear development involving steady promotion and increased responsibilities. The researcher focusing on the subjective career asks questions about how individuals see problems and possibilities; how they cope with and negotiate constraints and make use of opportunities; what they would perceive as the main influences, the key events, decisions and turning-points. This perspective informed the collection of the careers history data.

Life- and career-histories

Chapter 1 explained how the study of the subjective career was associated with interactionist theoretical perspectives which focused on career *action* rather than career determinants. Interactionist perspectives had revived interest in certain relatively neglected *methods* of research such as observation, participant observation, the use of autobiographical accounts and personal documents such as diaries and letters as sources of data. Of most importance to the present study was the revival of interest in life-history and biography. The work of Faraday and Plummer (1979), Goodson (1981, 1983, 1991) and Bertaux (1981) had succeeded in re-establishing life-history as an important source of sociological data.

The use of life-history material does entail certain difficulties, however. There is no set of tried and tested research techniques that can be taken up and adapted by any researcher (Sikes, Measor and Woods, 1985). The data has weaknesses as well as strengths. Problems of validity as well as of generalization have been considered (Bertaux, 1981; Corradi, 1991). Life-history data is particularly appropriate, nevertheless, for the study of subjective careers. Beynon (1985) claimed that life-history could fill in the huge gaps in our understanding of career, professional and personal lives. He argued that life-history data had advantages at three levels: subjective, contextual and evaluative. On the subjective level, life-history data was uniquely placed to attempt to understand the individual's subjective reality because it emphasized the interpretations that people place on their everyday experiences as explanations of behaviour. Contextually, Beynon claimed that life-history grounded the individual life in both the context of lived experience as well as the broader social and economic system in which they lived. The evaluative advantage of life-histories was in reasserting the complexities of lived experience for individuals rather than focusing on mass phenomena which could only amount to simplifications and generalizations of such individual complexities. Beynon claimed that life-histories could explore and build-up sensitizing hypotheses and concepts and that such data could correct, test and extend existing theory. He concluded (p. 177):

Life history material can tell us much about the socio-historical, institutional and personal influences on a career. It can help locate [professional work] in a wider temporal and inter-personal frame-work, incorporating external events that have diverted career trajectories (e.g. chance domestic factors or changes in the national economy) and pinpoint crucial benchmarks and phases in a career.

Other arguments in favour of using life-histories have been developed by Abrams (1982). He argued that the process of becoming and the process of social reproduction are one and the same. He also suggested that in contexts where the determining weight of external forces (e.g. structural determinants) appears to be overwhelming, the methodological argument for small-scale, detailed, qualitative research became strongest. Thus research into individual careers enables analysis to be done with sufficient detail to disclose what Abrams called the processes of becoming. The detail attained, and the complexity and variation of experience revealed, discouraged reification and structural determinism. It enabled researchers to see social reality 'as process rather than order, structuring rather than structure, becoming not being' (Abrams, 1982, p. 267).

It is possible to argue, then, that life-histories are not just interesting stories about particular individuals. Rather, the life-history is also the data of social history. Life-histories contain important information about social processes. They concentrate on process, rather than structure, which is an improved theoretical model since change is incorporated. The diversity and complexity that life-histories reveal enable researchers to avoid unduly simplistic models of structural determinism and actor passivity. The variability of actual experience, which is so important in postmodernist thought, is clearly demonstrated in the complexities of life-history material.

Arguments such as these were the justification for the use of personal histories in this exploration of gender and career in science and engineering. Complete life-histories were not used, however. Rather, the focus was the adult lives of the women and men, concentrating on their school and particularly their post-school experiences, at work and in their personal lives. Thus the interviews are referred to as *careers* history data. The intention was to collect details of each respondent's work and personal history and map these out so that different aspects of the career were interrelated. By gathering information on 41 subjective careers, it was hoped to say something about subjective careers in general. The individual narratives did indeed contain recurrent themes and general issues, making it possible to identify similarities and essential differences in the respondents' experiences of subjective career.

The research was not intended to produce statistical generalizations, however. Mitchell's observations (1983) on the epistemological basis of qualitative research (e.g. case-study and situational analysis) could also be applied to the careers history material. She argued that such research relies 'on the validity of the analysis rather than the representativeness of the events' (p. 190). Thus the experiences of the scientists and engineers in the careers history study may well be representative of scientists and engineers in general. But no claims will be made about their typicality. Rather, the aim is to increase knowledge and understanding about careers in science and engineering in industrial organiz- ations and about the variability in those experiences.

Data collection

The careers history interviews were conducted in 1991 and 1992; the en- gineers' interviews were completed first. The interviews usually took place in respondents' own homes, although a few were carried out in offices in one of the workplaces or in my own office or home. Evenings were the preferred time, although some respondents were kind enough to give up their lunch- times or even their free time at weekends. Interviews took between one-and- a-half and three hours. The interviews were semi-structured to ensure coverage of the same themes and, at the same time, to enable the respondents to determine the depth, range and extent of coverage of issues, as well as to add their own. The approach was thematic (Glaser and Strauss, 1967) and themes were allowed to emerge from the respondents' accounts of their ex- periences. In all cases, interviews were tape-recorded with the consent of the respondents and then transcribed.

The respondents were selected as far as possible to represent all the promotion levels (see later) in the two industrial organizations. Respondents were identified using snow-balling techniques and early respondents were asked to make initial approaches to subsequent respondents which greatly facilitated gaining access. It is inappropriate to talk of sampling, however, other than theoretical sampling (Glaser and Strauss, 1967) and no claim is made that the respondents' views are representative of some larger popu- lation. The objective was to understand subjective careers and career action, rather than to produce statistical generalizations about gender and career position.

The group of 41 professional scientists and engineers was unusual in that three-quarters of them were women. This over-representation of women was deliberate since the exploration of women's experiences of career in engineer- ing and science in industry was under-researched. The examination of gender differences in career in such contexts was also one of the objectives of the research. The non-representative nature of the group of respondents does not invalidate any conclusions about the nature of particular groups or of the way the groups might differ. The only thing that is precluded is straightforward generalization from sample percentages to percentages in the population (Abbott and Sapsford, 1987). Such a generalization will not be undertaken.

Organizations and respondents

The high-technology engineering company, Airmax, and the consumer pro- duct-manufacturing company, Marlands, both had hierarchical career and promotion structures for their professional (i.e. graduate) engineering and science employees.

For the graduate engineers working at Airmax, the career structure comprised a technologists scale which had four promotion levels. Following this were parallel professional and managerial ladders, each with three levels. Then, in promotion terms, there were the senior staff of the company and beyond that the directors and main board directors.

For the graduate engineers in this industrial organization, the ways to achieve promotion at the lower levels on the technologists scale were known; the criteria were understood and widely accepted. Between the four promotion levels there was a minimum wait at each level of two years. The criteria for promotion to the next level were clearly specified. Individuals who were able to fulfil such criteria and who had the support of their managers could apply for promotion to the next level. Beyond the technologists scale, there were differences both in the degree of openness and in the clarity of criteria for promotion.

Promotion on the professional ladder continued to be clearly specified and depended on work achieved. In that sense promotion was retrospective: individuals had to demonstrate they had operated and performed at a particular level before being promoted to it. In theory there were no number limits, although it was recognized that the company would not permit too many high-cost professional people to be appointed in any one section or department. The managerial ladder was more traditional, however. Here promotion depended on vacancies and the needs of the company. Management potential was less clearly specified, there was no minimum wait at any level and indeed it was possible to leapfrog and to miss levels should Airmax require it. This was also the case with the next set of promotion positions, the company senior staff. Here there was no system of advertisement or application; as with management positions, these posts were by personal invitation only. It was widely believed that only management posts could lead to these senior positions in the company.

The ages of the Airmax engineers in the careers history group ranged from 26 to 44 though the majority were in their thirties. Nine of the women and two of the men were on the technologists scale; three were in professional positions (two women, one man); four were in managerial posts (three women, one man); one man was company senior staff (there were no women at this position in Airmax) and one woman was a director (the only woman at this level in the company). The women in professional- and managerial-grade posts were virtually the whole population of women engineers in such positions in the organization.

For the graduate scientists and programmers working at Marlands, the promotion ladders were more variable. There were equivalent, standardized early career positions (scientist, senior scientist, principal scientist; or trainee programmer, programmer, analyst programmer, senior analyst programmer) where promotion was more or less automatic and regular assuming satisfactory performance. The senior positions here could involve managerial responsibilities but the next step, team leader, was the first recognized position on the complex managerial ladder. Further positions, such as section/project leader, senior section leader culminated in senior management posts such as head of section/department/process positions.

In a similar way to Airmax, early career promotions at Marlands were relatively easy to achieve. The criteria for promotion to the next level on the scientist or programmer ladders were more or less automatic, depending on fulfilment of specified criteria and satisfactory progress. The career ladder was more of a continuum, however, and it was claimed that individuals moved along it faster or more slowly depending on their abilities. A graduate straight from university would enter as a scientist (or trainee programmer) or perhaps a senior scientist depending on experience and the applicability of subject to the group. Those with PhDs would enter as a senior scientist or principal scientist if they had post-doctoral experience. Wherever a post involved management, however, candidates were required to compete with others for such positions. Senior management posts were filled by invitation only and here the criteria and the processes of application were less well-known. It was assumed that line-managers were the gatekeepers both to knowledge of and application for such positions.

The ages of the scientists and programmers in the careers history study working at Marlands ranged from 28 to 48 though, again, the majority were in their thirties. Six of the women (no men) were in the early career positions (scientist, programmer). Nine were in the lower and middle management positions of team leader to senior section/project leader (five women, four men). Two (one woman, one man) were in senior management posts. This left four women who were in management posts which were difficult to categorize. This was because of the complexity and variety of promotion ladders in this company where there had been less attempt to standardize career-promotion ladders than at Airmax.

The two industrial companies considered here constitute typical contexts in which engineering and science careers are constructed. In general, industrial organizations have three financial ways in which to reward and motivate their professional employees. There are also staff appraisal and continuing professional development schemes not considered here. The financial ways are by means of an annual (usually percentage) salary increase, merit pay schemes (usually for outstanding work performance) and promotion. The amounts available under the first two are influenced by the prosperity of the company and the negotiating arrangements and procedures between the company and staff, trade union and professional associations. These amounts will be reduced in years of economic recession and business stringency. The numbers of promotion posts and positions is determined by people-flow within the organization and by organizational restructuring. The promotion opportunities are strongly influenced by the supply of and demand for professional and experienced engineers and scientists. Promotion opportunities have to be maintained, however, if skilled people are to be encouraged to join and to be retained in the organization.

In both organizations, there were apparently no number limits (other than meeting the criteria) on promotions at the lowest professional levels (technologists, scientists and programmer scales). This was because of the needs of the companies to retain trained staff. The promotion criteria, in any case, posed a limit in that not all positions offered opportunities to meet the criteria (for example, designers do not often write reports – one of the stated promotion criteria at Airmax). It was likely, however, that in time blockages would develop at the top positions on these ladders. In this case, promotions criteria might need to be redrafted and renegotiated if the supply-and-demand factors for personnel became badly out of balance.

As Chapter 2 made clear, organizations form different career contexts compared with those of the more traditional professions (of law, medicine and academic science). Industrial organizations are also different from service organizations (such as education, health or finance and commerce) as contexts in which careers are built. The representativeness of Airmax and Marlands as industrial organizations cannot be assessed other than that they are both large national industrial corporations selling their products and competing in an international market. The careers of engineers and scientists working in smaller industrial organizations are likely to be significantly different.

The typicality of the careers history respondents' experiences is also difficult to assess, although they might be typical. The gender imbalance has been explained and hopefully justified. One other difficulty that needs to be accounted for is the lack of older respondents in the careers history group. In fact there are enormous difficulties in trying to locate women professional engineers and scientists who are aged mid-forties or over and who have spent all or most of their working careers in industry. In the 1960s, university engineering departments and women themselves did not consider engineering as an appropriate career choice. Similarly in science, although the exception here is biology as women have always achieved qualifications, if not careers, in the biological sciences. Most of the women scientists of the 1950s and 1960s would have developed their careers (*if* they developed careers) in schools or university departments or in personnel or other service departments of industry. Professional engineering and science work in industry and subsequent careers perhaps in management were effectively an all-male preserve.

Attitudes and actions began to change during and after the 1970s, as statistics from Women into Science and Engineering (WISE) demonstrate (McRae, Deyine and Lakey, 1991). Women's participation in such work (at professional and other levels) is now increasing, though it is an increase from a very low base. This gender pattern, however, creates problems for the careers history method used here. It is easy to locate men engineers and scientists of all ages who have constructed their careers in industry. It is relatively easy to locate some women engineers and scientists up to the ages of about 40. It is, however, very difficult to find women engineers and scientists at mid and later stages of their career lifecycles.

For this reason, the experiences of career of both older women and men have been omitted from this study. From what the respondents say, it seems that things are changing. But the extent of any change and the experiences of change must await later research, when women such as those considered here will, like their male colleagues, have spent most if not all their careers as professional engineers and scientists in industrial organizations.

Actions and structure

As the discussion in Chapter 1 made clear, career action and career structures are inextricably interrelated, mutually affecting and reproducing. It is necessary to end this methodological chapter by indicating how the subjective careers, the careers histories of the engineers and scientists, are used to inform analysis of career structures and contexts.

Each respondent in the careers history group had contributed a narrative, an interpretation, a self-conscious retrospective account of what they considered to be the important factors and influences in their own careers. When the narratives were read together, it was possible to detect similarities and essential differences in their experiences of subjective career. In addition, however, the respondents had supplied *information*: they had told of how they had got their jobs and their promotions, how they thought their organizations operated and how their own careers had developed. They had also explained aspects of the culture of their work as engineers or scientists working in industrial organizations.

The relationship between personal experience and social structure is a two-way causality, what Giddens (1984) called 'structuration'. The personal affects (i.e. reproduces or changes) the social just as the social constrains the personal. For any individual engineer or scientist working in an industrial organization, the career ladder appears as a given. The criteria required for promotion progress to the next level are the requirements, the conditions which individuals are required to achieve in order to progress or to continue in the current position. However, by working to match these criteria and meet the requirements, by applying for promotion and, for some, achieving the next position, individual actions are recreating and reproducing the career structures anew. Clearly there is little choice. Opting out would simply make it easier for others to achieve career promotion.

Career actions can alter structures, however, just as structures affect and limit actions. If sufficient individuals decline to relocate, refuse to take on additional responsibilities and resist promotion pressures, organizations will have to alter and adjust the promotion criteria or the career ladders themselves. Job specifications and promotion criteria and rewards do change when organizational requirements necessitate change. Similarly, the career patterns and trajectories of individuals will change as well as reproduce. Change is usually brought about by powerful economic actors within organizations who need to alter structures in order to respond to organizational needs and requirements. Career patterns themselves are changed by individuals responding to their own needs.

It is necessary, then, to understand the complex career processes that interact to produce career structures and influence career actions. These processes are primarily economic, but they are also cultural (gender, for example) and political (legislative changes and ideological beliefs) as well as functional and strategic (such as job descriptions and changes in specifications for particular positions). These are the processes whereby career structures become real so that individual engineers and scientists come to see their work, their lives and careers in terms of such structures. Careers are cognitive in that they are understood, experienced and negotiated.

This is the material used in the following chapters. The analysis will emphasize how careers are also normative in that they are constraining and limit choices of action. It is necessary to have constantly in mind, therefore, the mutually reinforcing processes of career actions and career structures; of how structures arise out of actions and how actions are influenced by structures. This is particularly important where change is affecting the organizations themselves, as well as the culture, structure and action dimensions of careers.

Chapter 4

Emerging Career Identities: Education and First Industrial Experiences

The extent to which individuals *choose* a career and *plan* career steps and promotion progress is very variable indeed. It is known that careers result as often from happenstance, procrastination and serendipity as from rational choice made from a wide knowledge base. But neither are careers *determined* in any clear way by background factors and circumstances. Although background characteristics can influence and constrain choice, individuals do nevertheless choose to an extent between the opportunities available to them. Careers most frequently result from earlier decisions which result in a narrowing range of opportunities. Career choices are also obviously limited by economic recession or increased by economic prosperity. Careers can result from coincidences and chance encounters, from family connections and the ties of friendship, as well as from organizational restructurings and changes in economic conditions.

For many individuals, however, the process of 'choosing' usually begins in the experiences and achievements in their school education. Those leaving school at the minimum leaving age of 16 are often destined for manual work or, increasingly, for no work at all, although Access and Open University courses as well as other training offer opportunities for older people to change career direction. Qualifications' inflation has increased the uncertainties of employment outcomes for those leaving education at the age of 18. Larger percentages of the age group are now continuing into higher and further education (about 30 per cent according to the latest figures) and increasing the aspirations of young people, if not the reality, for professional, managerial and higher-grade occupations.

How, then, does the process of becoming a professional engineer or scientist working in industry usually begin? The start of the process for many, including most of the careers history respondents, is the choice of subjects to study at school. The failure at this stage to choose maths and science effectively closes the door to professional engineering and science careers, as well as to many others. Changes *can* be made successfully later and career trajectories altered but change is more difficult the longer it is delayed.

In England, the long route to a career in professional engineering and science usually begins at the age of 16 with a choice of subjects to study for 'A'-level examinations (most commonly, three subjects are chosen). The choice used to be made even earlier with option choices for GCSE examinations made at the age of 14, although the introduction of National Curriculum requirements to study science and maths up to the age of 16 is postponing this critical decision. The effects of more recent changes to broaden and extend the sixth-form curriculum in schools (the introduction of NCVQ and Intermediate level examinations) are still too early to assess. These changes are unlikely to have any major effect, however, on the necessity to choose 'A'-level maths and science subjects in order to begin the process of becoming a professional engineer or scientist.

How, then, did some women and men, in the careers history group, begin the process of becoming a professional engineer and scientist working in industry? Before this can be considered, it is necessary to cover some preliminary groundwork on the issue of gender, science and technology in education.

Gender, science and technology in education

There are significant gender differences in subject take-up and specialization in schools in England, as in all industrial societies. Whenever choice becomes a factor and students are permitted to elect or opt for school subjects, gender differences emerge. Gender differences continue and are magnified in choices of subjects in tertiary education resulting in the inevitable outcome of occupational and career segregation by gender. This had tended to be represented as a problem for women, who thereby lose out in career opportunity, promotion and salary terms. Increasingly, however, it is being represented as a matter of social, economic and political concern, namely as a failure to recruit and develop half the population's talents in science and technology. In England, the DES Inspectorate have argued that 'the failure of many girls to acquire a broad education in the main areas of science means that they are deprived of essential skills and knowledge, and the nation loses scientific and technological expertise' (DES, 1985). This is not a problem confined to Britain. Other advanced industrial societies (USA, Australia, France) have commissioned research on the wastage of scientific and technological talent from women, when economic futures are seen as heavily dependent on manufacturing and information technology, scientific innovation and invention. The problem is not only one of access, but also of retention and progression. Educational institutions record a progressive loss of female enrolments in science and technology at each higher level of education systems (Kaminski 1982). The result of both access and retention differences is that there are fewer women in secondary science courses, considerably fewer in tertiary courses and only a small minority at postgraduate levels (Byrne, 1978, 1993; OECD, 1986).

There are, however, important differences within the sciences and technologies since these are not homogeneous categories. Byrne (1993, p. 7) has argued that although research in schools and tertiary education usually separates physics, chemistry, biology and maths, nevertheless the interpretations and generalizations and the policy implications drawn from the generalizations often refer to women in science and technology in unacceptably broad-sweep statements. Women are a tiny minority of students on mechanical, electrical and civil engineering courses in universities; their proportion increases slightly in chemical engineering. Women are a minority of physics degree students; they form a higher proportion of maths, chemistry and particularly biochemistry students; and they are a majority of biology and botany undergraduates. These gender-differentiated patterns cause Byrne (1993) to focus on the institution-based factors (the institutional ecology) of each discipline itself as one of the explanatory factors.

Other explanations have focused on the gendered imagery and culture of science, on territoriality, on peer pressure and on notions of gender identity and self-esteem. In feminist analysis these are linked with concepts of patriarchy and power (Hacker 1989, 1990). Researchers such as Keller (1982) have argued that the numerical preponderance of men, particularly in the physical sciences, has resulted in a male bias in the choice of problems investigated and how they are defined. Similarly Fee (1981) has alleged that objectivity (or traits such as rationality, logic and impersonality) is perceived as masculine and then endorsed as scientific. The opposite traits (such as subjectivity, irrationality, intuition and deduction) are ascribed as normally feminine. The associations of particular traits with one gender make it difficult for others to join without fear of loss of gender identity and self-esteem. Hence women who choose to study physical sciences risk a loss of femininity, at least by imputation.

Such explanations are persuasive but it is necessary to emphasize, again, that science is not homogeneous. Physics is regarded as normal for boys but non-traditional for girls – boys in the Girls into Science and Technology (GIST) project were labelling girls of 11–13 who did physics as 'a bit peculiar', according to Smail et al., 1982, as quoted in Byrne, 1993, p. 22. The complete reverse applies in biology. However, as Byrne (1993) demonstrates, women enrol more easily, more frequently and are retained in greater numbers in pure science and maths than in subjects such as engineering which are applied. Technology is even more problematic as a subject area for women. Research evidence from a range of industrial countries demonstrates that fewer girls enrol in applied sciences, fewer in applied than pure maths and fewer in technology-based subjects. Technology and engineering therefore pose a particular problem. Historically the image of engineering has been tough, heavy, dirty and to do with machinery. These cultural images remain powerful, although in the two World Wars (Braybon, 1981; Summerfield, 1989) neither women themselves nor their employers had difficulty associating women with these images. The contemporary image of professional engineering is undergoing change. For graduates in engineering there is now less emphasis on heavy engineering and machinery and more focus on computers, mathematical models, printed circuit boards and electronics. The gendering of engineering is still, however, very slow to change.

How, then, did the respondents in the careers history group perceive and account for their own early decisions in the education process that resulted in them becoming professional engineers and scientists working in industry? Two early influences are explored: the later stages of their secondary school education and their first experiences of industrial work.

Educational influences

In this section, the focus is on the key events in respect of educational experiences which influenced the careers history group of respondents to begin the process of becoming professional scientists or engineers working in industry. The events include the educational choices made and the school influences, both positive and negative, which were perceived. These influences are the ones the respondents themselves considered to be important. Not all the influences were important for all the respondents and where differences emerge they will be identified and explored. Some differences emerge between the engineering and science respondents; other differences are gender-related.

The influence of education and schooling on career decisions and choices has always been regarded as important. In quantitative statistical research, education is usually measured by indices such as type of school, length of education, examination passes and level of education achieved. These factors are then correlated with subsequent career achievements. In qualitative research, however, such as the careers history study, it is more the *experience* of schooling which is considered important. The careers history respondents were asked to assess the importance of their schooling in their emerging career choices. Four influences were identified, which are considered in turn:

1 the choice of subjects for 'A'-level study;
2 the positive experience of maths and/or science;
3 the effect of careers advice;
4 the influence of mentors and contacts.

Choice of subjects for 'A'-level study

The critical importance of choice of subjects for 'A'-level study on future career decisions has been recognized for a long time. Until the development of the National Curriculum, the English education system had allowed early specialization, as when pupils at age 14 had opted or elected to take particular subjects and to drop others completely (Pratt, Bloomfield and Seale, 1984). In the careers history group, Ann (a programmer) explained how the selection system, which her secondary school operated, resulted in her 'choosing' to concentrate on maths in the sixth form:

I took two maths and geography. I was good at maths. I couldn't think of anything else I was good at and there weren't too many other things, other than sciences, which you could take with maths that fitted into the timetable. So geography was the third one.

We had to decide at 14 whether to specialize in sciences or languages. That year I got a particularly grotty mark for biology so I did not make the science grade; I went into a language grade therefore. I had not done physics which was not too good for applied maths but you couldn't really do the chemistry without the physics. So it was decided at 14 really. (Ann, programmer)

Students are no longer required to make as many difficult choices at the age of 14 and the requirements of the National Curriculum necessitate a broad coverage. Choices *between* humanities and *between* languages still have to be made, however. The critical point of specialization now comes at the age of 16 when students move into sixth forms to begin 'A'-level study.

Changes are currently under way in England to extend the range of qualifications available for 'A'-level study in schools. The growth of B Tech and National Vocational Qualifications (NVQs) will expand the options for the growing number of students staying on in education beyond the minimum school-leaving age. For the respondents in the careers history study who stayed on at school, however, 'A'-level GCE subjects were the only option. A choice between subjects was possible and for the most part the respondents had chosen maths and science subjects. For the engineers, maths had been required, either with further maths and/or with physics and chemistry. All the five programmers (three women and two men) had studied maths and further maths. The scientists had more often studied three sciences (physics, chemistry and biology), although some had substituted maths for one of the sciences and two scientists had studied other subjects (geography in one case, sociology in the other).

Decisions about 'A'-level subjects were perceived as personal choices, however. The respondents chose their subjects because they saw them as interesting, more challenging and because they had done better at them than in other subjects. In general the schools were perceived as having had little influence on these choices (other than timetable restraints which imposed particular combinations of subjects). The respondents were not encouraged to take particular subjects, nor were they discouraged. For the most part the schools were perceived as entirely neutral in this important decision. Enjoyment of a subject was most influential and preference for particular teachers could also play a part:

The choice had to be made, shall I go for sciences or shall I take English and French or that sort of thing. I did very well in my 'O' levels so I could have done anything really, but I really enjoyed sciences so I just thought chemistry, biology and maths. I didn't do physics at 'O' level because for some reason I wanted to do history and there was a clash.

Also the teachers who teach you are an influence as well. The chemistry teacher was really lovely and the biology teacher was really nice as well, and the maths teacher was a sweetie, so I think I was just enjoying those classes more than others really. (Christine, scientist)

Because I have always been mathematically minded, it runs in our family. My grandfather was a superb mathematician, so I really enjoyed the mathematical side of it. Physics appealed to me because my school teacher was probably one of the best teachers I had ever come across and he was superb and got my interest going. I was advised to take four 'A' levels on the basis of what I had done at 'O' level and chemistry fitted very nicely and I always enjoyed chemistry anyway. (Philip, programmer)

I had always wanted to do sciences. I found the sciences more interesting and I was better at it, which is always a good basis for choosing a career, choose something you are good at. (Anita, engineer)

Most of the careers history respondents had stayed on at school to take 'A' levels; all of the scientists and programmers had stayed on at school but the engineers had been more variable. Four out of the 15 women engineers and two of the five men engineers had left school at age 16. All the respondents who had stayed on had perceived the choice of 'A' level subjects to be a personal one. For the most part, future career did not influence their decisions, although there were some exceptions:

To tell you the truth I don't know at what stage I wanted to be a vet. It was certainly before I was seven. I have always wanted to do it and I always told people that was what I was going to do . . . . I studied science and languages for my options at 'O' level so I didn't do geography or history or anything like that because I had to fit in the right amount of science, and then three sciences for 'A' level. (Marie, scientist)

I don't think I ever considered anything other than engineering – which wasn't an obvious choice at my school. I was supposed to do law; it was very much a classics grammar school; it started off as a public school. I did physics because I was good at physics and I wanted to do physics. I did maths because it was quite clear I was unlikely to get 'A' level maths and therefore the HND was open to me if I had studied maths to 'A' level. I did technical drawing because

I can just do that; I was always a dead-cert for getting that. I needed two 'A' levels to get my grant so it was minimum effort really that got me there. (David, engineer)

Whilst I particularly liked arts, I actually didn't find them very challenging. A lot of fun, but I felt that I would prefer to study the sciences because they were more challenging and keep arts for fun. At the same time I was also very interested in reading engineering and obviously I needed sciences to take a degree in engineering. (Frances, engineer)

A clear idea of a future career at the age of 16 was unusual among the respondents and this is probably also the case for most 16-year-olds. There was as much evidence of career happenstance as career choice and planning:

I wanted originally to study medicine. I started the first year (in the sixth form) wanting to do biology, chemistry and physics. To do the physics course at the school where we were, we had to take the first year of the maths 'A' level. I was absolutely hopeless at physics, so I went on to do maths.
    I didn't get a place (to read medicine). I was offered a place at Leeds to do combined bio-chemistry and physiology, I think it was, and rather than wait I thought I'd try it through UCCA (Clearing System) and if nothing came of that, then I'd wait until the following year and then reapply. But I was offered a place at Aberystwyth to read microbiology, which I had always been interested in actually. At the University of Wales there was this idea that you could have entry to medical school if you wanted to. So it was keeping the options open all the time. But I didn't change. I stuck with microbiology. (Eileen, scientist)

A choice of 'A'-level subjects, which in England usually involves a specialization in three academic subjects, was a choice which was perceived by the careers history respondents as being left to individual preference, while being constrained by school timetabling arrangements. Yet an 'inappropriate' choice for sixth-form study could effectively close the door on a whole range of occupations and careers, unless individuals were determined enough to retrace their steps in order to acquire preliminary skills and qualifications.
    Although not an issue for the careers history respondents considered here, gender differences in subjects chosen in schools have been noted in research findings. In particular, researchers have reported lower proportions of girls, compared with boys, choosing to study maths and particularly the physical sciences after the age of 16 (Kelly, 1981; Stanworth, 1983) and there have been several attempts to address this issue (Kelly, Ed., 1987; Pilcher *et al.*,

1988). As a result, subject choices in higher and further education are also significantly differentiated by gender (Thomas, 1990) and, hence, occupational and career segregation continues to be reproduced. The women in the careers history group *had* all chosen science and/or maths for 'A'-level study. In terms of choice of sixth-form study, all the respondents had emphasized personal preference in the decisions. In this respect, there were no gender differences noted in the responses.

Positive experience of maths and/or science

The importance of early experiences in critical subjects such as maths and science was identified by all the respondents as highly significant in the beginnings of development of their career directions. For the men respondents this was an easy identification to make. The transition into the maths and science streams of sixth forms was the confirmation of subject interest and preference. Sometimes first-choice preferences had to be modified because of timetabling constraints, but the moves were made easily and smoothly:

> I actually wanted to do maths, biology and chemistry but the curriculum wouldn't let me. Biology and chemistry were my two greatest loves of the sixth form and there was a lot of maths in chemistry and biology, but the school wasn't organised to do it so I did physics instead, which was a problem. (Nicholas, scientist)

Even where important changes were necessitated, these were operationalized with little difficulty and again happenstance was important:

> I was good at maths and I enjoyed maths – you tend to enjoy what you are good at. In the school I was in, you had to make a decision after the third year as to whether you were going to be science-biased or arts-biased. I actually intended to go down the arts route at that stage because perhaps I was slightly better at history and geography than I was at chemistry and biology. I did retain physics and of course I did maths. I took nine 'O'-levels and got eight – the one I failed was physics . . .
> The deputy head of the school was a maths graduate himself so he was keen for people to do maths, but in that school maths had to be science-based. That meant I would have to do physics because that was the only science I had. I had failed physics so I had to go to the physics teacher who was a new chap and say would he be willing to take me for 'A' level even though I had failed my 'O' level. He said yes, the course is not fully booked, yes we will have you. So that is how I ended up with double maths and physics. (Arthur, programmer)

Most of the women respondents in the careers history group had been high achievers in maths and/or science and this early success and recognition had been important in marking the beginnings of the process that eventually resulted in science or engineering careers. For the women engineers and programmers, their early experiences in maths had been particularly important:

> I was always good at maths. I found it easy when most of my friends didn't. I suppose that encouraged me. (Wendy, engineer)

> It was always something that I was good at. I always found it very easy to work with numbers, to remember formula. I could memorise formula and know how to apply it and, to me, that was what maths was all about. I found it incredibly easy because it was just about applying formula to numbers and out popped the answers. (Alison, programmer)

Experiences in maths were also important for the scientists. Julie was fortunate in her school's science provision and equipment, but she also identified her experience in maths as of particular importance:

> I went to a grammar school in . . . which was an all-girls grammar school with the most fantastic science labs. When I think back on it now I think that must have been part of what crystallised it all. It was an all-girls school so there was no competition from the boys and we had all science mistresses and these beautiful laboratories, very well equipped even by todays standards. Also, having separate maths lessons with no boys in the class, and a very good maths mistress, and I think that gave me the push into science. (Julie, scientist)

Not all the women had had positive experiences of success in maths, however. Two of them had recognized the importance of maths but had had to battle with their schools in order to be able to continue their studies. Lindsay, with her father's support, had succeeded in persuading the school to allow her to continue with GCE 'O'-level (first stage) maths rather than CSE which was widely considered a lower level qualification. (Both these certificates have now been combined into the GCSE (first stage) certificate.) It is interesting to compare Lindsay's experience with that of Arthur reported earlier:

> The maths was a very big thing because at that time there was a big struggle for me to do 'O' level maths. They (the teachers) were saying you've got to do CSE just based on one result in the third year of school. I was a bit border-line and we had to really struggle.

Lindsay had succeeded and had gone on to do GCE 'A'-level in maths, physics and geography and had followed this with a degree in aeronautical engineering. Ann had been less successful, however. Her early experience of lack of success in maths resulted in her taking humanities at 'A'-level:

> At the end of the fifth form I wanted to do maths and science. I think the maths grades went from grades one to six and I only got a two so I was deemed not suitable to do 'A' level maths. And if you can't do 'A' level maths, then you can't do any of the sciences. So I ended up doing history, geography and French and my heart wasn't in it. So I eventually passed 'A' level geography and not the other two.

Ann left school at the age of 18, joined Airmax and eventually succeeded via laboratory work, day release and evening study, to complete a Higher National (HNC) in maths which enabled her to progress in an engineering career.

Early recognition of the importance of critical subjects such as maths at school, and preferably success in such subjects, are extremely influential therefore in keeping open access to choices of sixth-form study. In their secondary schools, if young people learn by whatever means that they cannot do the maths, then certain job choices and careers in professional engineering and programming are effectively closed.

Careers advice

Once in the sixth form and embarked on some combination of science and maths advanced study, then eventually decisions about what to do after school had to be made. All except two of the careers history group who had taken 'A'-levels had proceeded straight to university or had taken one year out between school and university; one woman programmer had studied maths as part of teacher training. For this group, university was automatically perceived as the next step, particularly for the scientists though less so for the engineers. Career-planning seemed to play little part in the choice of subject, however. For the most part decisions were made to continue to study subjects, or combinations of subjects, which had interested the respondents in their 'A'-level studies. Of the 15 women in engineering (both those going straight to university and those entering employment who were later sponsored by their employers to undertake degree or equivalent qualifications), only three had chosen to read for an engineering degree. Of the other 12, five had studied for degree or degree-level qualifications in metallurgy; seven had studied maths, chemistry or physics at tertiary level. For the five men engineers (again both those going straight to university and those doing degree or degree equivalent qualifications after employment), two read for engineering degrees (one in engineering metallurgy and one in metallurgy) and one in economics and materials.

Of the three women and two men programmers, all but one (who had studied economics and econometrics) had done tertiary-level qualifications in

maths, sometimes with computing and statistics. The women and men scientists had studied for degrees in either biology, biochemistry, microbiology, chemistry, pharmacology, pharmacy, zoology or combined science.

The careers advice which the respondents had received at school was largely perceived as having little impact. There was information available, but those going on to university were assumed to be able to postpone future work decisions. Those who were unsure about careers (the majority) were advised to keep their options open.

> We had careers interviews at school. We had quite a good careers service; there was a lot of information available that you could browse through. In the interviews we were told to keep our options open unless you were really positive there was something you wanted to do. (Fiona, scientist)

> I had three or four job offers and because of that I was not expected to stay on. The careers officer at the time was of the attitude – you've got a job, you should be pleased with that. So I left school. I wasn't given any advice at all to stay on. No encouragement to stay on. (Peter, engineer)

> I don't remember the careers officer in the school having any influence on my choice (to read maths). Perhaps it was 'What do you want to do? University. Oh yes that's fine. Next person please!' (Arthur, programmer)

There were gender differences in this experience, however. Where the men in the careers history group were unaffected by the lack or otherwise of careers advice, some of the women had perceived any advice as positively unhelpful. Cultural perceptions of what is appropriately men's and women's subjects and careers had affected any advice they had been given:

> I went to see the careers master and he asked me which teacher training college I was going to and when I explained that I wasn't going to teacher training college, he said what are you going to do? I said that is why I have come to see you and he said why don't you join the army. So I said thank you and left. I got no advice whatsoever. (Julie, scientist)

> There was very little careers advice in my school because the careers mistress happened to be head of English. If you were interested in science she didn't really want to know. She just said well there's the filing cabinet, dears, go away and look. (Sylvia, scientist)

Several of the women had been high achievers at school and, as a result, particular educational choices and traditional career routes were encouraged. One of the respondents, Sarah-Jane, remained bitter about her experience:

> I was a very shy, introverted, naive child . . . I was quite prepared to sit for Oxford and Cambridge in my second year. But, in fact, something happened which even the school's wildest dreams had never led them to expect, which in fact had an adverse effect on me. I got a scholarship to Oxford. I wasted a year of my life sitting the third year in the sixth form. The Oxford course was four years, as opposed to a three-year one at Cambridge. So that took two years out of my life, just like that, besides landing me up at Oxford as a rare creature – female – which coloured my relationship with men. (Sarah-Jane, scientist)

> In fact I originally applied to university to do medicine, not with any special conviction. It wouldn't be fair to say I was pushed into it, but it was a fairly normal thing for a clever girl who was good at sciences to do. In fact I missed getting one grade in my maths, which is the reason for having the year off. (Jennifer, scientist)

> I almost made the mistake of thinking about medicine, slightly pressurised into it by the school, they tried to twist my arm to be a doctor. You're bright. If you're bright be a doctor and about 15, 16, I thought hard on that line. (Mary, engineer)

The women engineers found careers advice particularly unhelpful. Most of the women who had continued into higher education read for maths or pure science degrees, which corresponded with their schools' expectations. Only three of the women moved on to take engineering degrees, five had studied metallurgy, sometimes going against the school advice they had been given. For some of these women, the lack of knowledge of industry or engineering, or cultural prescriptions in careers advice, on the part of their advisers in schools was problematic. It posed a handicap, hindrance or delay in the development of their engineering careers.

Mentors and contacts: teachers and others

Individual teachers and other contacts had sometimes been important in providing information, support or encouragement. Again there were some gender differences. The women in the careers history group referred to such forms of assistance whereas the men had not. The women had received particular, individual, help and encouragement which seemed to be important. Advice and real support had come from particular teachers and from other (family) contacts.

There was one particular member of staff who was the senior mistress and she supported me and pushed my other tutors into saying 'Yes, we will give you extra tuition to get the (grades you need)'. . .

I was sent to a couple of vets at the age of 15, to our local vet and another quite a long way away who my parents knew very well, to be put off. And having *not* been put off they were extremely helpful and supportive, and they encouraged me all the way. (Marie, scientist)

The local pharmacist, who ran the shop around the corner from us, knew I was doing science 'A' levels and came to the house to talk to me about it. It was my mother who set it up. She used to spend a lot of time in the chemist. They just got talking and he said he would come round and have a talk. That is how it happened really. (Lilian, scientist)

A friend had a pharmacist father and I was absolutely intrigued by pharmacy and, I thought, I want to do pharmacy. (Pauline, scientist)

The women engineers, in particular, were dependent on such forms of encouragement.

But then once I got to 'A' level and was doing physics and maths, there was a chap who did metal work, he took metal work at school. He was really keen, he wanted to encourage people to do engineering and he did an awful lot. Just out of interest I did machining work, just an hour a week, just to have a go and get some feel for it. He also got me a couple of weeks in an engineering company in . . . just to have a look round the areas. (Lindsay, engineer)

My chemistry teacher thought I should do chemical engineering and my physics teacher, who was an ex-chemical engineer, thought that chemical engineering would be very good. They encouraged me. (Anita, engineer)

I was lucky in that I had a very good relationship with my maths teacher in the sixth form and he hadn't got any fixed ideas about what women ought to do. In fact he said ignore what the headmaster's saying, do what you think you want to do and as long as you enjoy it, that's what matters. He had worked for British Nuclear Fuels as an engineer, after graduation, and he happened not to enjoy it so he went into teaching. But he thought people ought to at least try what they think they want to do. (Wendy, engineer)

For the women in engineering, individual teacher influence, support and encouragement were frequently referred to. These were teachers who had experience of industry and engineering and they were able to convince some of the women at least to consider such careers.

In general, then, for the respondents in the careers history group, their early experiences of critical subjects such as maths and science were positive and influential. These experiences perhaps marked the beginning of their subsequent careers in engineering and science. The women's experiences were more mixed than the men's. For most of the women, their early experiences with maths and science were positive; they were high achievers. For two of the women, however, battles with their schools over maths for one woman reinforced her determination but for the other resulted in an inappropriate choice of 'A'-level study and a delay in recognition of what she wanted from her career.

For the careers history respondents, the choice of maths and science at 'A'-level, which was perhaps the most critical decision for their subsequent careers, was perceived as a personal choice. The schools were not seen as instrumental either way in this decision. The respondents had chosen out of interest, perceived aptitude and because those subjects were seen to be more challenging than others. A future career, for the most part, was not seen to be important in the choice. Careers advice was mostly perceived as unhelpful, certainly as unadventurous especially for the women. However, particular teachers, usually themselves in science or maths and often with industrial experience, were perceived as important influences by the women in their emerging and developing career directions.

First experiences of industrial work

For the respondents in the careers history group their first experiences of industrial work had been important in their choice to develop their careers in industry. Their first experiences had been at different ages and stages in their educational careers. Four women in the engineering group had left school at 16 and one at 18. Two of the men engineers had left school at 16 and one at 18. They had undertaken engineering or laboratory work in industry and had subsequently, through industrial sponsorship or day-release and evening study, worked towards their degree or equivalent qualification. For the other respondents who had gone to university straight from school, their first experiences of industry, either through sandwich courses, vacation work, conferences or industrial sponsorship, had also been very important. In these cases, however, their experiences had followed on from their subject choice at 'A'-level. For most of the respondents this was the critical first step. However, their experiences in industry clarified and confirmed the career direction they would subsequently take.

Of the four women who went into engineering work in industry after leaving school at 16, leaving school was perceived as a positive decision made by the women themselves. They were inclined towards laboratory work and they resented the stereotypical job choices they were being guided towards at school.

> I think while I was at school, I didn't want to teach, I think that that was one of the first things that I thought I would do. I wanted something that wasn't ordinary. You will see that all the way through – nothing ordinary (laughter). (Kate)

> I left with no aspiration other than to leave school, because I got fed up. I didn't want to work in a building society or be a nurse or a teacher, which was all the advice I got. I knew I wanted to do something different. I wanted to be a computer programmer but they told me my maths wasn't good enough. So then I said I'd go and work in a lab and just applied to (several companies) and it just so happened Airmax came up with the job first. (Alice)

For the women who had joined Airmax without higher education qualifications, the move into professional engineering was subsequently assisted by Airmax's policy of offering and encouraging further education and training. The young women recognized the need to acquire further qualifications for career progress and they were able to convince their managers to support them. For the men engineers who had moved into employment without higher educational qualifications, all had been sponsored by employers other than Airmax. Later they moved to Airmax to develop their careers.

For the other respondents in the careers history group taking 'A'-levels in the maths and sciences, the next move into higher education was not perceived as a choice so much as the automatic next step. The decision about *what* to study was important, however, and here chance encounters and organized conferences sometimes played a part in influencing particularly a decision to undertake an engineering degree.

> I don't know what happened, either I had got the wrong day or something happened but it was an open day for production engineering. I think I was the only person who turned up that day, and I had a wonderful time and within a few hours of looking around the department and understanding what constituted production engineering, I was completely hooked and I thought this is exactly what I want to do and it was so clear. (Frances, engineer)

> I was very idealistic like all 17 year olds, I wanted to save the world and stop the war in, sorry the 'troubles' in Northern Ireland, and reduce pollution and improve the environment and stop famine in Africa. I found that there were some people talking there who had done wonderful things to improve the environment and had made better food manufacturing processes and cleaned up some rivers.

And they were all engineers; they weren't scientists, they were chemical engineers or industrial engineers or mechanical engineers or electronics engineers, and it suddenly dawned on me that engineers existed. (Anita, engineer)

Both men and women respondents, scientists and engineers, spoke positively of their first experiences of industry.

I decided that I would do a sandwich course so I would get better experience and understanding of how things worked. The industrial experience gave me the opportunity to work in various parts of the country doing things which were really different from each other. It was terrific . . . They were all very different and I'm glad I've been through them all. (Paul, scientist)

I took the job at . . . in my year off and during that year that was when I really decided that I enjoyed practical lab work immensely. So that was a very influential time. (Jennifer, scientist)

Between school and going to university, I worked in a company call Chemray, and they cross-linked polymers by radiation and I had a very enjoyable three months summer in there, the first taste of industry. I tried to electrocute myself daily; that was quite enjoyable. I was testing end seals on insulators, putting them in water then putting a current through them and so I was able to look at polymerisation then. (Mary, engineer)

For other respondents in the careers history group, work experience while at university had confirmed the direction their careers would take. This was particularly important for those undertaking maths or pure science degrees; their experiences of industry while at university were critical in influencing their career choices.

I knew I didn't want to do accountancy or go into the financial sector, but apart from that I had no idea at all. So I took this about ten-week summer job and you were just given basic jobs to do, but it was the 'hands-on' hardware and try and understand the hardware, what the results were telling you and trying to fit models to it, that I thought this is an area that I want to go into. (Beryl, engineer)

The first encounters of these respondents with industry were remembered as particularly important in their emerging and developing careers. For those women and men who left school at 16 or 18, an inclination towards laboratory or engineering work guided their job applications. They pursued such openings following advertisements or family connections and the women were not swayed by notions of more 'appropriate' work for women. Once in such jobs the women and men recognized the importance of educational qualifications for career progress and were able to convince their managers to send them on day-release programmes to acquire their degree-level or access to degree-level courses.

For those respondents, women and men, who went straight on to university (or after one year out), either to read for maths, engineering or science degrees, their first experiences of industry and engineering and science-work practices were perceived as extremely important in their developing identities as industrial engineers and scientists. For the women engineers, the recognition that engineering existed as a profession could be revelatory (see Anita) since they had encountered nothing like it at school. The realization that engineers did not wear dirty overalls or repair machinery, but rather worked at computer screens or in offices and in meetings and discussions with colleagues was a critical experience.

For women and men respondents it was the work cultures and practices of science and engineering in industry that were attractive. The appeal of 'solving problems' and 'working problems through' were frequently mentioned. The procedures and the practices of *doing* science and engineering and the discussions about applications and processes were appealing. The work was not boring or repetitive; there were always new applications and projects. The 'hands-on' experience and the production of 'results' were what made the work attractive in the eyes of these respondents. Their career objectives were becoming clearer.

Conclusion

This chapter has explored the beginnings of the process of becoming a professional engineer and scientist and working in industrial organizations. It has examined the experiences of the later stages of education and the first encounters with industrial work of the careers history respondents.

For all the respondents who had stayed on at school, the choice of what to take for 'A'-level study at the age of 16 in school sixth forms was probably the start of the process which eventually resulted in careers in science and engineering. Some respondents had effectively made choices at the age of 14 when choosing options for first-stage examinations. At the start of 'A'-level study, these respondents had chosen various combinations of mostly maths and science subjects. Their choices were perceived as individual preferences; they had chosen according to perceived interests, aptitudes and abilities. According to the respondents, their schools had played little part in influencing this choice; the schools were perceived as essentially neutral. Schools had sometimes influenced their combinations of 'A'-level subjects, however, because of timetable constraints on choice.

There were few differences between respondents at this stage of the careers process. Those who eventually became engineers or programmers had more often chosen maths, whereas several of the scientists had studied three sciences: chemistry, physics and biology. There were no gender differences in the perceptions of individual preferences being the main determinants of choice at this stage. Clearly, though, if 'preference' itself is gender-related, choices will be affected – though this could not be examined in the careers history study since these respondents *had* all chosen maths and/or science.

Most of the respondents had had positive experiences of the subjects of maths and science: they had been high achievers. This was not the case for all the women respondents, however. Four of the women had left school at 16, one at 18. This group had worked for Airmax and had returned to education, either full- or part-time, and had eventually become professional engineers. Two out of this group had had particular problems with being allowed to study maths. So, even for the high achievers, there were some gender differences in experience. For the men respondents, their positive experiences in science and maths led them automatically, even unthinkingly, to move into 'A'-level study of these subjects. For the women, however, such a move required a clear decision, a positive choice.

The perceptions of the respondents in respect of careers advice had been seen as mostly unhelpful. There had been plenty of information but use of this material was left to individuals. As most of the respondents were destined for university, it tended to be assumed that decisions about careers could be postponed. There were gender differences in the experience, however. The men respondents had few expectations in respect of careers advice and were content to make their own decisions concerning tertiary-level courses. Several of the women respondents found the advice they received to be unhelpful, restrictive and culturally prescriptive. This was particularly the case with the high achievers, where Oxbridge and/or medicine were argued for strongly and persuasively.

The influence of mentors and contacts, teachers and others, was also gender differentiated. The men respondents did not refer to such sources of influence. Some of the women, however, remembered positive support, encouragement and advice mostly from individual teachers: significant role models who were remembered as especially influential. Other contacts, often connected with their families, were also sought out, consulted and used.

For all the respondents, their first experiences of industrial work were important influences on their subsequent career directions. Eleven of the respondents (four women and five men scientists; one woman and one man engineer) had achieved doctorates; academic careers would also have been possibilities. Experiences in industry, often doing research-related or project work, were perceived as preferable contexts for careers, however. Such work was experienced as more directly relevant and important. Scientific and engineering work in industry was perceived as more secure (compared with the short-term contracts that were an increasing feature of academic careers), offering more opportunities for varied work and promotion progress. Their work in industry involved solving problems, devising procedures and processes, testing and coming up with results. A promotion move into a management post was a promising possibility. Their careers could be developed in such contexts.

The theoretical perspective explained in Chapter 1 requires the linking of structure, culture and action influences in the analysis of stability and change in careers. It is necessary, then, to emphasize that career 'choices' are not determined in any simple, one-way direction by background factors and other circumstances. Although background and structural characteristics influence and constrain choice, individuals do nevertheless to some extent choose between the opportunities available to them. A theoretical debate about occupational choice took place in Britain in the 1970s between researchers advocating rational and conscious choice and those asserting more deterministic allocation (reported in Dex, 1985). In the 1980s it was recognized that occupational placement was complex and included aspects of choice (Willis, 1977; Sherratt, 1983) as well as of determinism. Feminist analysis contributed to this position in examining how, for women, aspects of culture and structure interrelate to affect 'choice' itself.

The experiences of the respondents in the careers history group confirm that the career process is complex. Aspects of structure constrain choices as well as outcomes. The actions of these respondents in their educational decisions and early industrial experiences had begun the process of career development. The interrelation of aspects of the organization, as well as aspects of public and private lives, must now be examined in order to assess how these factors influence, change and sometimes reproduce the processes of career.

Chapter 5

Professional Identities and Work Cultures

There is a long tradition of research in sociology on occupational and professional socialization, on the processes of becoming a worker of a particular kind and of being in the sense of having a particular occupational identity. There is also a long history of research on the cultures of particular kinds of work, on the details of everyday working routines and practices, on the manner of dealing with work tasks, on the categorizations of clients and customers, and on relations with colleagues, officials and other professionals. In general, these approaches attempt to 'tell it how it is' to become and to be a worker of a particular kind. This theoretical tradition was inspired by the Chicago School of symbolic interactionists (Hughes, 1937) and some in this tradition have studied the processes of becoming and being much more widely than in occupations. As Johnson (1983) has claimed, researchers have studied the processes of 'becoming' in respect of patienthood, deviance, criminality and sexual difference. This chapter uses these theoretical models to consider the professional identities of engineers and scientists working in industry and to examine their work cultures and perceptions of their day-to-day work routines and practices. It also assesses to what extent gender was a significant differentiating factor in work experiences and the processes of becoming. It asks how different were the day-to-day experiences of engineering and scientific work in an industrial organization for the women and men in the careers history group.

Professional identities

The concept of professional identity needs some preliminary explanation. There has been considerable research into occupational identities both in the sociology of work and the professions. From early studies of men and their work (Hughes, 1958) and of professional socialization (e.g. Becker *et al.*, 1961; Lacey, 1977), it was established that work identity – that is, how individuals are placed and place themselves in their occupations – has a profound effect on their thinking, attitudes and actions. Strauss and Becker examined adult socialization as a process of identity formation: 'central to any account of adult identity is the relation of change in identity to change in social position' (1975,

p. 95). It is suggested that mature adults know themselves through their work and social identities. Work, career and gender identities are fundamental aspects of adult socialization. This chapter considers the effect of professional work and gender identities on perceptions of self. It explores how different attitudes to work and experiences of it are reflected in the experiences of the women and men in the careers history group.

Science and engineering

The professional identities of scientists and engineers working in industrial organizations are developed in different ways compared with their colleagues in educational institutions such as universities. The work of scientists and engineers in industry has always been constrained by commercial considerations. In the past this was less true of academic scientists and engineers where 'pure' research could be justified in funding applications. Conditions have changed in universities, however, and the applications (and commercial exploitations) of research, and sometimes industrial sponsorship and joint funding, are increasingly required.

The university model of science still influences and offers a role model, however, particularly for scientists (rather than engineers) working in industry.

> I probably write more reports for publication than I do for internal consumption. One of my jobs is to maintain the academic profile of the department. (Michael, scientist)

> I'm involved in a programme of research looking into finding new drugs for arthritis. I'm a biologist so I'm not involved in the synthesis of compounds but in testing them. So that would be identifying important points of control that have relevance to the pathology of the disease, setting up models which can test those points of control, then running the programmes for testing the drugs ... Then of course I'm responsible for writing it all up afterwards and sometimes trying to get it published. (Jennifer, scientist)

The scientists in the careers history group did emphasize certain differences between their experience of scientific work and that of university scientists, although the differences they perceived are probably exaggerated and the scientific research work done in universities is perhaps idealized.

> If we talk about academic scientists they would look at a particular system and would probably study in depth for a long period of time and they will want to know to the last detail what made it tick or try to. In many ways we are using what other people find and apply it to

our own particular purposes. We do novel research that we believe has not been done before and we publish what we believe to be novel information, but I don't think that anyone of us would classify ourselves as being primarily pure research. (Paul, scientist)

Indeed, it is likely that many university scientists would envy Susan's position:

Then I have my research which I do myself and I have about one-and-a-half technicians doing research for me full-time. It has all got to be towards depression; working out what causes depression . . . I would discuss it with my more senior manager . . . and I've never had anything I wanted to do turned down yet. (Susan, scientist)

For the engineers in the careers history group, the university model of engineering was of less interest or concern. For some, their university education was perceived as far removed from real engineering work. It was the hands-on experience and practical application of engineering principles which was significant to their professional identities. However, there was some concern about the status of engineering for their professional identities and the academic stamp was perceived as important in enhancing that status.

Engineering is difficult because of the problem that anyone can call themselves (an engineer). If we define engineers as someone who is professionally qualified and chartered, then academically you stand on a par with a doctor or a lawyer or whatever. I think the frustration is status. People will tell you it's the salary, but I think on the whole it's status. The fact that the man who comes and mends the fridge for you calls himself an engineer. (David, engineer)

For both the scientists and engineers in the careers history group, it was career development in their industrial organizations which most affected their professional identities. Career progress in both Airmax and Marlands required movement into managerial posts. This in turn necessitated doing less of the actual scientific or engineering work and more of the management of those doing the technical work. Movement up the managerial ladder was seen to involve a reduction in scientific/technological input but an increase in the ability to facilitate what other people were doing. A manager had to assign priorities and the further up the managerial ladder, the bigger the decisions. Managing people involved a lot of paper work, decision-making and administration and less hands-on experience of science and technology. Their scientific or engineering backgrounds, however, were crucial in enabling them to make the right managerial and administrative decisions.

I would put myself as a scientist and as a manager. I have quite clear scientific duties. I read the scientific literature. Then there is straightforward management and that really is running one's eyes over test results to make sure other people have done the right things with them. (Paul, scientist)

I would call myself a technical manager. My work involves managing suppliers and controlling the product they supply. I ensure, monitor and control the quality of the product supplied, be it from a dimensional point of view, be it from a chemical point of view. (Andrew, engineer)

There were some differences between the scientists and engineers in terms of the effects of management on professional identities. The engineers seemed more willing to relinquish their professional engineering identities in order to perceive themselves as technical manager (Andrew), operations manager (Edward) or group manager (Kate).

In contrast, the scientists were more interested in maintaining their scientific professional identities even when their work entailed significant managerial responsibilities:

A scientist more than a manager. I would describe myself as a microbiologist really. (Sarah, team leader)

A scientist first, yes. (Eileen, quality control manager)

I would still describe myself as a research scientist. (Nicholas, senior section leader)

It is difficult to explain this difference other than by reference to the status issue already identified (see David earlier). The career route out of engineering into management in industrial organizations has been identified as a problem of professional identity for engineers (Finniston, 1980). The notion of their particular expertise is in any case unclear since their knowledge base and skills are wide and diverse. Then, when such expertise diversity is compounded by career promotion into management, the problem of professional engineering identity is intensified. The same problem of professional identity for scientific managers is not experienced, however. Career scientists who are promoted to managerial positions in industrial organizations continue to perceive themselves either as both scientists and managers, or as scientists first and foremost.

Gender differences

There were significant gender differences in the way professional identities were experienced by respondents in the careers history group in their industrial organizations. For the men scientists and engineers, their gender was unproblematic in their experiences of professional identity and organizational career. They perceived themselves to be scientists, engineers and/or managers working in industry and that was sufficient. For the women in the careers history group, however, their gender could be significant in their experiences and perceptions. They were perceived as, and experienced themselves to be, *women* scientists, *women* engineers and *women* managers. In this respect, their gender was a crucial aspect of, and had to be incorporated into, their professional identities as well as into their career ambitions (see Chapter 6).

Previous researchers have focused on aspects of women's experiences of being female in their work roles. Some of this research will be referred to here, before considering the accounts of the women in the careers history group. Thus, Schwarz-Cowan (1979), Cockburn (1985) and Hacker (1989, 1990) have examined the difficulties for women in engineering. Byrne (1993) and King (1994) have outlined the problems for women's careers in science. Savage and Witz (1992) and Wilson (1995) have reviewed the gendered aspects of career and work in organizations. There is also a growing literature on women's particular difficulties in management positions which will be referred to in Chapter 8.

According to Schwarz-Cowan (1979) the difficulties for women in tech-nological occupations stem from the association of gender with particular cultural attributes and characteristics. A passage from Schwarz-Cowan (1979, p. 62) summarizes the polarization of characteristics which are attached to gender in the processes of socialization:

> While we socialize our men to aspire to feats of mastery, we socialize our women to aspire to feats of submission. Men are hard; women are soft. Men are meant to conquer nature; women are meant to commune with it. Men are rational, women irrational; men are prac-tical, women impractical. Boys play with blocks; girls play with dolls. Men build; women inhabit. Men are active; women are passive. Men are good at mathematics; women are good at literature. If something is broken, daddy will fix it. If feelings are hurt, mommy will salve them. We have trained our women to opt out of the technological order as much as we have trained our men to opt into it.

Cockburn (1985) has endorsed this polarized characterization and has argued that when men and women, things and jobs, comfortably reflect such gender-differentiated values, order prevails. However, when women undertake male work, such as engineering, they upset a widely accepted sense of order and meaning. She has asserted (1985, p. 12) that 'technology enters into our sexual identity: femininity is incompatible with technological competence; to feel technically competent is to feel manly'. It is also the case that the cultural processes of gendering are immensely powerful and that individuals suffer if they go against such cultural dictates. In this way Cockburn argues that engineering itself will present women with cultural dilemmas. To do engineering work seems to present responsibilities and role expectations which, as women, they find difficult, if not impossible, to fulfil.

The writings of Hacker (1989, 1990) have had a rather different focus. Following her own experiences of engineering education, Hacker explored how the pleasures of making things work are turned into processes of domination. She examined the links between gender and engineering in military institutions and organizations. Hacker's writings, therefore, encourage a focus on the processes within institutions and organizations whereby engineering is made into a mode and a form of domination which is a male-only preserve.

The particular problems women experience with science and with science-occupations have been reviewed by Byrne (1993). The problem is more complex, she says, than the school processes of boys' territoriality, sex-appropriate labelling and peer pressure or self-esteem. Again the difficulties are perceived as cultural and associated with polarized gender characteristics. These polarized characteristics are then incorporated into institutions and organizations and into structures of political and economic power. Thus, according to Byrne, the alleged 'objectivity' of science is ascribed as a masculine trait and then endorsed as scientific. The 'subjective' is ascribed as feminine and the associated traits (intuitive and deductive, personal and irrational) have no scientific standing. According to Fee (1981) these differences have been institutionalized structurally within the sciences themselves: the physical or hard sciences such as physics are most scientific while the soft biological sciences are most descriptive. Science is also part of a male-dominated power structure which has economic and political implications. In addition science itself is biased, since only certain problems are investigated while others are ignored (Keller, 1982).

Rather different 'cultural' aspects of science are examined by King (1994) who explored scientific reputation-building as a cultural construct. King used the example of Rosalind Franklin to demonstrate how reputations are very far from being straightforward reflections of scientific achievements or publications' productivity. Although King's analysis was concerned with academic science, the idea of reputation-building also has resonance to the construction of science careers in industrial organizations. Reputations and careers in organizations are similarly constructed by means of gendered rhetorical resources and processes.

Research such as this encourage a focus on cultural processes in general but also on the way organizations work and use gender to structure work, promotion potential and career processes. There has been growing interest recently in Britain in the ways in which gender and organizational processes interrelate and interact. Savage and Witz (1992) have reviewed the theoretical developments which have resulted in gender in organizations having a prominent place in contemporary social theory. From the early focus on bureaucratic organization, feminists have moved the discussion to how those bureaucracies are gendered. Similarly, Wilson (1995) has critically examined the myths (such as differences rooted in biology and the idea that women and men are polar opposites in motivations, aspirations and abilities) that surround women at work in organizations. Instead she offers the realities of working life for women (low pay, part-time work, family responsibilities, gendered appraisal and promotion processes) as a more appropriate explanation, all of which realities stem from organizational structures and mechanisms.

A number of interesting questions emerge from the research literature, therefore, and these can be addressed in a preliminary way by reference to the experiences of the women and men in the careers history study. What were their experiences of professional scientific and engineering work in large industrial organizations? What, in their view, were the difficulties they faced in their day-to-day work? Were the women's experiences significantly different to the men's?

The women, like the men, in the careers history group for the most part enjoyed their experiences of scientific and engineering work in industry. There were gender differences in their experiences, however, and there were significant differences between the women themselves. Not all the women had problems in reconciling their gender and professional identities in the organization. Frances, the most successful in promotion terms of the women and men in the careers history group, had experienced no difficulties in her career. Already a director at Airmax, being a woman had been irrelevant to her engineering career:

> I haven't felt at a disadvantage ever. Some people can be patronising, but I don't think I'm conscious of it except when a third party has made a comment about it. You know, 'That was a patronising comment, wasn't it?' and you think well was it? Yes it probably was, but it just washes over me, it really doesn't affect me, so I probably don't see it. Perhaps it's there. (Frances)

Like Frances, other women felt they had been able to take advantage of being female and thereby get themselves noticed in the organization.

> It can be very much to your advantage to be a woman. In (my area) you are a novelty because more often than not I am the only woman at a meeting. It can work to your advantage once you have got used to it. Sometimes you think you are a bit of a sideshow: you are sent places because you might make people more comfortable than a man would . . . That is an advantage for your managers. But I don't think it has been a big disadvantage to me. (Penny, scientist)

Other women in the careers history group, however, *had* experienced difficulties. These ranged from the casual remarks or questions at interview to the apparently well-intentioned body-touching:

I was asked 'How much mileage can we expect out of you as you have just got married and are likely to have children?' I get sexist comments but I give as good as I get and I don't consider that to be sexual harassment. I have never been chased around the lab although I know people who have. (Marie, scientist)

It depends on what you mean by sexual harassment really. A lot of people find our boss quite offensive because he's very tactile and I think he's tactile with a lot of people. You know he'll give you a hug or a squeeze or whatever. He knows that people generally won't say anything like 'Please don't do that. I find it offensive', so he'll carry on doing it. I think there is an abuse of power sometimes. (Christine, scientist)

For other women, gender relations at work were a significant difficulty and the experience was often a surprise as well as a problem. Sometimes experiences were graphically described and would certainly be accurately designated as sexual harassment. For the women engineers, particularly, their experiences of harassment intruded into their professional identities at work.

I have been surprised that there are difficulties in discrimination and people. I don't know what you would call it, it's not sexual abuse, but you do have problems at work because you are a woman and the way they treat you. I never even thought about that, I always thought it was people making it up, or people just asking for it. But it is a problem, and I've found it difficult because you can be doing your job and you have got to go to these people to do the job and they can wield . . . Just because they make you feel uncomfortable it can be a problem. I have been surprised at it, you don't get it at university and you don't get it with your own age group; maybe because you can handle it better, you speak the same language. But it's the older ones and they are probably the ones who have the authority over you, so I don't like that side. (Lindsay)

I've had someone try to kiss me in the stores; I have had someone try to help me up into an engine in a rather too familiar way; I've had wolf whistles; I've had people deliberately give me the dirtiest heaviest jobs; I've had an ex-military policeman flick pieces of swarf at me until I went and stuffed them down his shirt; I've been leered at. I've had the embarrassment of going into a hotel with my manager and people making all the jokes – 'Are you going to sign in as Mr and Mrs Smith'. I've walked onto a military base and been just glared at by a load of scientists who worked for the American Air Force, who cannot believe that a little girl is saying these things. At the end of me giving a serious talk to a designer, I've had – 'It's a pity you have got blue eyes isn't it, I prefer women with brown.' I've been patted on the head. I think being a woman and being very small and looking like a little girl has made it worse. (Anita)

In general the experiences of the women were variable. None of the women had experienced problems with the scientific or engineering work as such. They could manage the science and the technology and play a full part in the culture of science and engineering work. Similarly, some of the women disclaimed any difficulties within the organization. Being a woman was irrelevant in some experiences of day-to-day work. For most of the women, however, their gender was problematic because it had to be additionally incorporated into their identities as professional scientists and engineers in the organization. The experience of such difficulties either necessitated some resolution or the living-out of dilemmas and contradictions in their daily experiences at work.

Work cultures

Work cultures consist of the day-by-day work routines and practices which are undertaken by workers of particular kinds. Knowledge, expertise and experience are operationalized differently in each work setting and particular work cultures have been described in offices, laboratories, factories, classrooms, hospital wards, consulting-rooms and shops. Researchers have been concerned to describe the creation, transmission and reproduction of such occupational knowledge (Coffee and Atkinson, Eds, 1994). Others have made important distinctions between the technical skills or expertise required to be a worker of a particular kind and the habitus (Bourdieu, 1988) or indeterminate facets of an occupation which have to be acquired but are never explicitly taught (Atkinson and Delamont, 1990). Such indeterminate facets have important gender consequences if women do not get the same opportunities as men for learning the habitus of occupations.

Science and engineering

The scientists and engineers in the careers history study had all been asked to describe their work and to list their work activities in a typical working day in their industrial organizations. There were some similarities in the work activities of the scientists and engineers in the early promotion positions, on the scientist or technologist salary scales. Their work primarily involved the application of standardized scientific procedures and testing techniques to compounds, components and materials. Some, usually the more senior, were involved in actually designing the test systems themselves.

The main function for which I am paid is to look at the tissues that are derived from safety studies on new potential medicines . . . The tissues are sent to my department where they are processed and cut into very thin slices which go on to slides. I look at the slides and write a report, and that is arguably the most important part of my job. (Marie, scientist)

The work I am doing at the moment is standardisation. In the first part, where we are looking at critical parts, we get information from material supplies. You are making judgements on the information, based upon experience and standardizations that have gone on in the past. You have a long list of what you have to do, so you actually work through your job list with those parts on. The second part is to record the information within reports and make some recommendations. (Peter, engineer)

A lot of the time it's looking at mechanical property data and relating that to the failure mechanisms of it and the reasons why they've failed. (Nigel, engineer)

My work is to design biological test systems which will discover model chemical enmities for the treatment of skin and heart disease. (Paul, scientist)

Principally it is involved in setting up new methodologies for use in several project areas. (Michael, scientist)

The application or development of standardized testing procedures was an important aspect of the experience of work of both the scientists and engineers in the careers history group. To that extent, their working days were structured and formalized; the content of their day was predictable. Their work responsibilities had been allocated and prioritized; their achievements could be reported, monitored and assessed.

The scientists and engineers were unanimous in their real enjoyment of the everyday tasks their work involved. The most favourable aspect was 'the production of results' which gave satisfaction as well as giving each individual a ready measure of job achievement. The aspect least enjoyed was 'the writing up' which was perceived as necessary but boring and tedious. They perceived their work to be varied, novel, interesting and challenging. The work culture and practices of doing science and engineering were attractive. The appeal of 'solving problems' and 'working to solve them' were specifically mentioned by the engineers. For the scientists, the appeal was more the testing techniques and screening procedures themselves which were meaningful. For both scientists and engineers, the procedures and practices and the team discussions about applications, processes and practicalities made their work interesting. There were always 'new applications and new projects', and different issues to be 'measured, assessed and resolved'; new ways of working and reworking old and recurrent problems.

For the scientists and engineers with managerial responsibilities, their work involved the direction and administration of their sections and teams. The managers were generally clearer about their responsibilities than about their daily activities, and this is probably an effect for this group of the need to readily produce CVs, job descriptions and appraisals. Miller and Morgan (1993) have explored how the CV comes to be experienced as the job or as the person. The senior managers, in particular, rehearsed a number of responsibilities and their daily work routines were much more difficult to characterize.

Currently my role involves managing a group of approximately 200, covering a multiplicity of disciplines from materials, mechanical testing, specimens of a smaller scale to large component testing, arrangements on experimental machine shops, materials data generation, to materials research for metallics, materials analytical methods, and an operational management role . . . My standard day's pretty fluid. A high degree of meetings around a number of subjects; thinking time which is very important to me, but a high degree of personal contact as well, with my team, customers; it might be one-to-one, by telephone or by direct meetings or it may be a large forum. (Edward, engineer)

The meetings and discussions, by telephone or by one-to-one contact or in small or larger groups, played an increasingly large part in the experiences of work of those who achieved successive promotions in their careers. Their scientific and engineering expertise crucially influenced the decisions they were making, but their *direct* experience of such scientific and engineering work declined. The managers were increasingly dependent on others to supply data and assessments. Their job was to assign priorities and to determine directions as well as acting as intermediaries between directors and middle-managers.

Gender differences

The women's experiences of scientific and engineering work in the two industrial organizations had varied. Some of them denied any differences from their male colleagues, either in their own experiences or in their treatment by others. For most of the women in the careers history group, however, their experiences of science and engineering work in the organization were different to their male colleagues, as were their work relations. Their experience of difficulties (see pp. 76–7) necessitated some response from the women in their daily experiences at work.

In a study of women in managerial and professional organizational positions in Canada, Sheppard (1989, p. 146) described a strategy of 'blending in and claiming a rightful place'. Such a 'blending' depended on very careful management of being feminine enough (in terms of appearance, self-presentation, acceptance of different expectations and of motherhood responsibilities) while at the same time being business-like enough (competent, desiring promotion to a point and in particular directions) in order to claim a rightful place in the organization.

For the women scientists and engineers in the careers history study the management of gender in the organization was seen to lie in their own hands and was perceived as being related to 'personality'. The women's experiences illustrated two techniques. The first can be termed 'fronting-it out' and the second 'playing the little woman'. These responses were perceived not so much as a choice for individual women but more as reactions and responses determined by personality and type of character.

The response of 'fronting-it out' involved confronting the problem as a challenge and having the 'personality' to do it.

You've got to front it out. You either pinch their bottoms back, wolf whistle back at them! I had the joke: 'Do we have to have so-and-so on our section he's not pretty enough, I like prettier men on our group'. You do it back to them and they soon give up, but you've got to have the strength of personality to do it. I've seen women pushed into corners because they haven't got the personality to do it and not given the chances. (Anita)

You find your own tactics to sort them out. Either you get them to one side and say, 'Look, I'm not into all these jokes', or you tell them they are behaving in a sexist manner. If things don't work, you try put-down techniques in front of other people, and that generally works. (Vivian)

You have to be fairly confident and you have to be fairly outgoing. You've got to be prepared to stick up for yourself and not be walked over. If you do that, there are no problems. (Beryl)

I get a lot of sexist comments but I give as good as I get. (Marie)

I'm actually seen as some sort of abnormality really because I refuse to conform and wear feminine clothes. Because I cycle, I just go to work in jeans and even though I'm in a senior position I don't see the point in wearing very smart clothes if I'm doing lab work all the time. I think I'm treated differently to other females within the department, because I'm more one of the lads really. (Christine)

Such a response was not without problems, however. Sheppard has graphically described the precariousness of managing gender by confronting any challenge head-on. 'A woman who does not appear to be or to act "feminine" enough . . . may find herself perceived as "too masculine". Such a definition is negative and may result in the use of labels that are seen as punitive, such as "lesbian" or "castrating bitch" ' (Sheppard, 1989, p. 148). A related problem is the consequence of such perceptions for career and promotion in the organization. Managers had expectations of professional employees and such expectations were gender specific. Women who 'fronted-it out' might be perceived as confrontational, or as too aggressive for the 'cooperative' team work required in the organization.

The second response which the women engineers described was to 'play the little woman' and again this was seen to depend on 'personality'. This response involved tolerance, even acceptance, of gender challenges and not provoking confrontation. It might also include the use of feminine tactics such as tears and 'getting upset', either real or imputed (in general the tactics of the weak and dominated) as a perceived response:

There are instances like that where I feel you've got to control yourself. Because to suddenly fly off and react would be seen as a weakness and I would see it as a weakness. (Mary)

I'd say that if you've got a tolerant, cooperative sort of nature and you're female in the Company, you're more likely to survive than if you try doing things the men's way. It's unacceptable really for a female to join in with the lads and swear at them and that sort of thing. If you go about things the way a man would, you loose their respect because they don't want you to be . . . they want you to be one of them in certain ways, but not in others. I suppose some people would say they are old-fashioned, but they have certain expectations. (Wendy)

I mean there are one or two instances where people have said – when I have been in a discussion, not a heated discussion, but we obviously have disagreed on odd occasions, and one of my previous managers did say to me that I mustn't get so upset, and I said, I am not upset. I was just putting my point of view forcibly, not aggressively, but I was getting as forceful as he was at me. But because it was me, he used the word 'upset' and I took exception to that and I said 'If I had been a man you wouldn't have used that word, would you?' He actually had the guts to admit that he wouldn't have. He said, 'No. Looking back, I think I used that because you were a woman.' But at least he was able to admit it. So I think there are these preconceived ideas that sometimes come out. (Carol)

Again, such a response entailed serious difficulties. The male-dominant culture of science and engineering could not entertain elements of perceived female weakness and submissiveness. Doing science and engineering involved working in teams and being able to argue a viewpoint 'forcefully and emphatically'. Similarly there were serious difficulties in terms of career and promotion in the organization. To 'play the little woman' risked being assessed by management as weak and passive, lacking in promotion potential and being judged as unsuitable for career progress and development.

There was another resolution, however, and this was generally preferred. Most of the women argued that it was necessary to be a *good* scientist or engineer. By building a reputation and earning respect, the contradictory expectations could be avoided. Again, the solution was perceived to lie in the hands of individual women; they had to be particularly able scientists and engineers.

> I find that the engineers will go very much to Rob rather than to myself and what I have to do is build a reputation for myself really; and earn their respect. I do analysis for them and sort out problems as they come up and basically you've got to be twice as good and it is built on reputation. (Amy)

> The main thing is that you've got to show that you are competent to do the job and if that's the case, then people just accept you. (Beryl)

> Generally once you are known as a person they accept you, if you know your business, but if you don't then you are lost. Whereas people are prepared to accept some young male engineer who isn't particularly good, they aren't prepared to accept a woman engineer who isn't particularly good; there is much more fuss made about it. (Anita)

> On the shopfloor you've got to win respect. You've got to be seen as a competent person. Males get that respect when they start, but females have to achieve it. (Mary)

Most of the women in the careers history group saw 'building a reputation' to be the best strategy for women scientists and engineers in their organizations. Nevertheless, problems and difficulties remained as the women themselves recognized. The problems were particularly related to career and promotion development in the organization. To 'build a reputation' and be a good scientist and engineer was extremely difficult in organizations where career and promotion were competitive and where there were numerous highly motivated, achievement-orientated individuals in competition for every promotion post. Managerial assessment and appraisal was also critically important for career progress in organizations and managers continued to be influenced by gender-related expectations and assumptions (see Chapter 8).

Conclusions

This chapter has examined the professional identities and work cultures of women and men scientists and engineers in the careers history study working for two large industrial organizations. It has assessed the similarities and differences between the scientists and the engineers and it has analysed gender differences in the experiences of such work.

The scientists and engineers shared many aspects of their work cultures. Their work primarily involved the application of standardized scientific procedures and testing techniques to compounds, components and materials. Some were actively involved in designing such procedures. Results were then required to be written up into reports and submitted to team and section leaders and managers who used such reports in decision-making about operations and future projects. Promotion into management positions required individuals to do less of the scientific and engineering work and more administration of team-work.

In terms of professional identities, some differences were observed between the scientists and engineers. The engineers seemed more willing to relinquish their engineering identities in favour of promotion positions in management. In contrast, the scientists were more interested in maintaining their scientific identities alongside of, or even despite, their managerial position. Both groups were, however, concerned to emphasize their *particular* scientific and engineering specialisms in their identities as, for example, microbiologist, cell biologist, vibration dynamics engineer, composite materials engineer. The labels scientist or engineer were perceived as insufficient to indicate their professional interests and concerns.

The experience of gender differences was varied: the men and some women in the careers history group had no difficulty in incorporating their gender into their professional identities. Other women *had* experienced difficulties. Problems arose because of aspects of gender in their industrial organization, not because of the technical cultures involved in the scientific or engineering work itself.

The women varied in their experiences of gender problems in the organization. Some denied any difficulties while the experiences of others ranged from contractory expectations that were difficult to reconcile, to overt sexual harassment and other forms of gender-joking. The women attempted to resolve such gender problems either by 'fronting-it out' or 'playing the little woman'. However, both these resolutions entailed difficulties in respect of career progress and promotion in the organization. A third resolution, which might be combined with the previous two, was to attempt to 'build a reputation' as a competent, even a 'good' scientist or engineer. Even this solution was problematic for women and career, however, since promotion was highly competitive and dependent on management appraisal. Managers in the organizations continued to have gender specific expectations of the professional scientists and engineers on their teams.

Researchers are increasingly arguing that it is necessary to investigate how gender is embedded in organizational structures and processes. The experiences of career of the respondents in the careers history group confirm the impact of organizational systems. It is important to understand more about the processes of career and gender in organizations. It is also necessary to understand the effects of other aspects of identity, however. Both women and men have other selves, other characteristics, responsibilities and relationships which are incorporated into and operationalized alongside professional identities. Some of these are examined in the next chapter.

Chapter 6

Careers and Families: Public and Private Lives

The previous chapter considered professional identities and how these were developed, maintained and sometimes changed by the women and men scientists and engineers in the careers history study. This chapter deals more specifically with career identities: that is, how the women and men perceived their work responsibilities had developed and would be developing over the course of their working lives and how they were responding to expectations for promotion in their professional career. More specifically, it deals with the coordination of public and private responsibilities in careers' histories and with the incorporation of personal aspects of self into the public domains of scientific and engineering work in industrial organizations.

The notion of career identity is relatively new. Banks *et al.* (1992), reporting the findings of an interdisciplinary programme of research on young people growing up in four areas of Britain, defined 'identity' as embracing 'the individual's own perception of himself or herself generally and in specific domains – for example, occupational identity, political identity, domestic identity' (p. 12). Extending this to the scientists and engineers, career identity is the individual's perception of self in respect of promotion and achievement in the positions and hierarchies of the work organization. It includes an examination of the different ways in which individuals negotiate and reconcile domestic, professional and career identities in the course of their working lives.

There are clear gender differences in the reconciliation of different aspects of social selves and career identities. The accommodation of gender, career and profession in the construction of social identity affects women in a very different way to men. Motherhood has a different impact on professional and careers aspects of identity compared with fatherhood. Fatherhood is compatible with continuing professional development and career and promotion achievement. Motherhood assumes a degree of detachment from a profession and a postponement of promotion in favour of childcare and other family responsibilities.

Sharpe (1984) has argued that in spite of a broadening in attitudes and increased opportunities in education and work, feminine identity nevertheless still involves marriage and motherhood and, in turn, these are assumed to affect profession and career aspirations. Work today has assumed a more central and continuous place in most women's lives; this was examined in

Chapter 1 (pp. 10 and 17–19). The large majority of women now work for a substantial proportion of their adult lives. The break for childcare is still common but even here more women than ever before are returning to work after the completion of their maternity leave (McRae, 1991). In this context, continuing in work or returning to work offer these women an opportunity to retain and develop a work identity separate from the home and family.

In this way, work has become part of women's identity and self-image and an important component of their relationships with their families and with people and institutions outside the home. But women's attitude to 'career', in the sense of promotion in the work organization, remains more variable. Work has, for example, resulted in a double load since family responsibilities continue alongside profession and work aspects of social identity. Sharpe (1984) has analysed this 'double identity', the constraints and the satisfactions, where women have a work identity in addition to their identity as wives and mothers. Increasingly, then, women's experiences at work as well as at home are important in shaping their consciousness and sense of self. It has been recognized that this dual identity might be reflected in their work-task performance and style. However, dual identity will not necessarily allow women any more time for themselves; usually it compresses their responsibilities into an even tighter schedule (Sharpe, 1984). Inevitably, this affects their attitudes to promotion and to taking on increased responsibilities at work. There is also a tendency, as McRae (1986) noted, for women to compensate for their occupational behaviour by retaining responsibility and control of housework and care responsibilities. 'Enactment of traditional role behaviour on the part of wives domestically [is] a way of ameliorating their very non-traditional behaviour occupationally' (1986, p. 141). In these ways, domestic work and care responsibilities might be women's way of asserting or re-establishing their femininity.

There are no equivalent cultural tensions or structural constraints affecting men's attitudes to career promotion. Increased work responsibilities and the associated increases in working hours and commitments are part of men's normal career development, together with the resultant salary rewards. Some men have always been 'reluctant' managers (Scase and Goffee, 1989) in the sense of resenting the increasing encroachment of work into family and private lives and there is some evidence that men in dual-career families are experiencing heightened conflict in respect of personal responsibilities (Thompson Thomas and Maier, 1992). In general, however, increased promotion and career commitment are part of the expected lifecycle development for men working in organizations. Indeed, this has necessitated the provision of career routes and rewards by work organizations in order to motivate male white-collar workers.

Public and private lives: the careers history respondents

The respondents in the careers history study were differently placed in respect of their private relationships and family circumstances. All 10 men were married; five were childfree and the other five had one or two children. The partnership arrangements of the women were more varied. Of the 31 women, 25 were married (12 engineers, 13 scientist/programmers), five were in partnerships (three engineers, two scientists) and one scientist was single. Thirteen women were childfree at the time of the interview (eight engineers and five scientist/programmers) although one woman engineer was about to have a first child. Eighteen of the women had between one and three children, most having one; and two of the women were pregnant with a second child.

It was also interesting to note the numbers of women in engineering, in particular, who were married or had partners doing the same kind of work and frequently working for the same organization. In fact 13 of the women engineers were married to or in partnerships with engineers; only two were in partnerships with non-engineers. Also, nine of the women engineers had husbands/partners working in the same industrial organization, though usually in different departments or sections; six had husbands/partners working for different organizations. This was not the same for the men engineers; none of their wives were engineers and all worked for other employers.

For the 13 scientists the pattern was more variable. Of the women scientists, four were married to or in partnerships with husbands in the same profession and discipline; eight were in a different profession (one was single). All 12 husbands/partners worked for different organizations. For the three women programmers, all three had husbands/partners doing the same kind of work and two worked for the same company. For the five men scientists and programmers, all five had wives/partners doing different kinds of work and four worked for different employers.

It has long been recognized that work organizations frequently also operate as marriage markets. The importance of universities as places where partnerships are formed was also endorsed by the experiences of the careers history respondents. At the same time, the difficulties (as well as the advantages) encountered by dual-career couples in the same profession have been reported. For the women engineers in the careers history study, the support might have outweighed the career competition. However, I have noted the difficulties for women in dual-career couples, where both partners were in the same profession (teaching) and direct career and promotions comparisons could be and were made (Evetts, 1993).

Negotiating dual-career arrangements

Marriages and partnerships affect the careers and career identities of women in a different way to men. Davidson and Cooper (1992, p. 150) have reported the findings of a study by Berger, Foster and Wallston (1978) of the job-seeking strategies of more than 400 young scientists in dual-career marriages. The study reported that, while most initial job-seeking strategies and some final decisions were egalitarian, the majority of final decisions were traditional, in that the husband accepted a job first and the wife followed him.

Similar patterns were also confirmed by the careers history respondents. Some of the careers of the men engineers particularly endorsed the traditional pattern.

> We were courting while I was at university. I think she had always resigned herself to the fact that when I got a job she would have to move. I started at Airmax in the September and she moved in June and was looking for jobs from when I started. She actually took a job that was a lot less money than what she had been on up North. (Nigel)

> We met at (university). I graduated a year before her so I was down in . . . for a year and then she graduated and came to join me. She worked for NatWest bank as one of their graduate intake. She was going on this graduate scheme that looks at pushing people. They are put through a very disciplined, very high pressure [scheme] sort of driving them into positions where they'll have responsibilities and really driving them hard into progressing into the management role. I think she decided that 1) there was the intention that we would have a family; 2) it's likely that she will stay with the children; so 3) is it worthwhile, with that in mind, continuing with this high pressure thing? . . . So she came to the decision that she really didn't want to pursue this highflying route with NatWest. (Andrew)

Not all the dual-career arrangements in partnerships were managed in the same traditional way, however. Some decisions were perceived as 'difficult' to make, even if the end result was the same.

> She decided to leave to join me. It wasn't easy. It was obviously helped by her working for one of the big four banks. The opportunity was there to move and stay with them. But it wasn't an easy decision. (Edward)

There were also clear signs of change both in attitudes and in arrangement. Change was illustrated particularly in the dual-career arrangements negotiated by some of the women scientists where husbands had agreed to follow their wives' career moves.

> Before we were married he was working for a company down in London, but when we actually got married he then looked around for a job in this area because I was working at Marlands at that time. (Sarah)

> He applied for a move to [this area] and as it happened they were crying out for staff [here]. It was a move for my career. He said it was my turn. (Penny)

I was very interested in a job in Australia which did not quite turn out the way I wanted it to, and we were both going to go and leave. [He] was quite happy to give up his job to go there. (Susan)

Changes in the negotiating and balancing patterns of careers in dual-career partnerships were apparent, therefore, particularly for scientists in the careers history group. However, partnerships continued to pose career constraints on both members.

I don't think he has got a lot of option now from the point of view that we are tied into things like school fees. We have had discussions at various points like when the first baby was born, when the second baby was born and the third baby. This is your last chance, do you want to go back to university because if so I had better start looking for another job. There were points when we could have made a change but I think it gets more difficult as your children get older because they get tied in to school and friends. It would be a terrible wrench. He has had the chance to do it and I have offered and he has said no. As far as I am concerned there are alternatives in the area, but I do quite like working for Marlands. (Marie)

It seems, then, as though the traditional pattern of women following in dual-career couples is changing and giving way to more complicated systems of mutual negotiation and dual support. Women might still 'follow' more than men, but some women are now negotiating with more confidence and more as equal partners in dual-career couples.

Changing patterns of childcare

In Britain many professional women still leave their work, usually between the ages of 25 and 40, in order to care for their own young children. This contrasts with the pattern in Europe where most professional women stay in employment when they have children. The pattern is changing in Britain. The break for childcare is still common but more women than ever before are returning to work after completing their maternity leave. The greatest numbers of women returning to work are in professional and managerial grade occupations where about 60 per cent of mothers with children under five are in employment (McRae, 1991).

The break for childcare is now frequently limited to paid maternity leave only. There is also more variety in the way couples manage domestic responsibilities. New divisions of domestic labour are beginning to emerge as in some partnerships both partners are developing careers. Gregson and Lowe (1994) noted new forms of 'between partners' domestic division of labour, as a consequence of the employment of waged domestic labour.

In the careers history group, 18 out of the 31 women, and five out of the 10 men, had children and childcare arrangements had had to be made. Options for childcare were limited, although for this group cost was not the overriding concern. It might also be the case that certain childcare patterns become established and used as preferences by individuals in particular professions and organizations. For example, for the women scientists working for Marlands, nannies were used by four couples although none of the women engineers used nannies. Day nurseries were used in five families, by women and men, scientists and engineers. The most frequently used option was probably the childminder, however; childminding arrangements were used in all families and had been used by some whose children were now attending school.

Of the three men engineers with children, two had wives engaged in full-time childcare. A decision by one partner of a couple to be a full-time childcarer was not confined to wives, however.

I went back after [my daughter] was born which was full maternity leave. My mother came to live with us until [my daughter] was one year old, by which time [my husband] gave up his job and looked after her full-time. He was a 'househusband'. Then [my second daughter] was born and I took a shorter maternity leave and at five months I left her at home and [my husband] looked after her until 18 months ago when the financial climate and his age suggested to him that he ought to be trying to get back to work before he was 40. (Julie)

New patterns of childcare were emerging, then, among these relatively privileged groups in employment terms, such as the women and men scientists and engineers in the careers history study.

Career identities

What were some of the ways in which women and men working as professional scientists and engineers in industrial organizations, and with the sorts of personal situations previously described, negotiated and reconciled their domestic, professional and career aspirations in the course of their working lives? What alternatives existed in terms of perceptions of self in respect of promotion and achievement in the career positions and hierarchies of the work organizations? In respect of career identities, four types were apparent. These were:

1 the single-focus career: promotion antecedence;
2 the dual-focus career: promotion accommodation;
3 the dual-focus career: parenthood accommodation;
4 the single-focus career: parenthood antecedence.

The types were differentiated in terms of several characteristics but the most important was the balancing of the private and the public aspects of the self in the construction of the career identity. The types were differentiated according to the prioritizing of aspirations for promotion in the career. Also different were the prioritizing of personal and career goals and the ordering of paid and unpaid work aspects of career. Related to this was the individual's self-image and what were regarded as the most important sources of identity and satisfaction with self.

The single-focus career: promotion antecedence

When career identity had a single focus and promotion was antecedent, the individual was clearly committed to promotion in the career. There was no attempt to balance different aspects of the self; instead the self was perceived primarily in terms of the promotion position achieved and where the next step might be. Work and career were the most significant aspects of self and the career identity had a profound effect on thinking, attitudes and actions. Where promotion was antecedent in the single-focus career, individuals were very ambitious for promotion and had very high aspirations for their career. Traditionally the single-focus, promotion antecedent career had been perceived as a male preserve. However, in the careers history group this was not always the case. Several of the women could be regarded as currently having a single-focus in their career and where promotion was antecedent. Four cases have been selected to illustrate this type of career identity among the women. Each of the four women was differently situated in respect of their personal relationships and promotion positions so far achieved, but all were very ambitious for their careers.

Frances was the most successful in promotion terms in the careers history group. At the age of 38 she had reached director level. She was single although she had been in a stable partnership for 12 years.

They know we have a partnership but it really doesn't interfere at all. I think we both have worked pretty hard to make sure that that continues. But no [he] has been very supportive. He really wasn't sure when I left Airmax because obviously he had seen my career move on pretty well in the company. But he was very supportive when I left and even when I contemplated the possibility of having to move to the States. Obviously that wasn't palatable, but I think he would have supported it. So I think he's been supportive, but indirectly.
J.E.: And you haven't ever felt constrained or restrained in making career moves?
Frances: No and I wouldn't. I think I made that sort of fairly clear from the start. I think as time goes on whilst that might be the objective I think it perhaps would get a little more difficult. One

never knows until it's put to the test, but I think that I am single-minded enough to say well it has to be like this.

J.E.: What are your hopes for the future?

Frances: Well I would very much like to sit on the Main Board of Directors. I don't at the moment see myself leaving the company again. I think it is unheard of to leave the company twice, [laughter] but for the right move I would. I think knowing now that I love [the product], I'm reasonably restricted to Airmax. If things went awry for whatever reason, be it my fault or not, then I would leave. But I would very much like to make Main Board and really as far as possible influence the future of our great company. That would be a real treat to have the opportunity to do that so I will have to work hard and keep my fingers crossed for a long time I think.

J.E.: You are obviously perceived as a career person, is this the correct perception?

Frances: I think it is yes, in fact I am sure it is. (Frances, no children)

Beryl was currently in a managerial position. At the age of 32, she also was single and in a stable partnership.

I had made it known quite clearly in Staff Appraisals that I wanted to get on in the company and that I wasn't prepared to stay as an engineer, I wanted to move up the managerial level as far as I could go. I am career-orientated. When this job came up, I felt reasonably confident about it because I had made very strong statements that it was an area that I wanted to work in, and I knew that I could do the interviews. So I was fairly confident that I had a good chance of getting it and I did, and that's where I have been for the past eleven months . . . Honestly, I won't make Chairman or Managing Director, but certainly I would like to get up to Company Senior Staff, middle to senior type managerial level and I've also got to widen my experience because I have been in a fairly restricted field. I'm getting a lot more visibility and I'm seeing a lot more of the Company now in my present job . . . I'm a career person. I don't intend to have any family. (Beryl, no children)

Amy was one of the youngest women in the careers history group. She was 26 and had worked at Airmax for only one year.

I am career minded. I think my husband would rather I wasn't. But I am. It's more important to me than family. I think my husband would prefer it to be a combination of the two. I think it's a case of see how it goes. At the moment, all I'm interested in is career, but my opinion does not get a hundred per cent hearing . . .

My aim for the next few years is to work at the next grade up. A year of building on the job and acquiring experience and then the next year of doing the next grade job. That way I can move every two years. That's my opinion. At the moment I am in competition for a Section Leader's job with a chemist who had been with Airmax for 10 years; I've been there one year. He has *only* worked for Airmax; I've worked in other jobs for nine years. I do have a different approach. I feel I get on better with people than he does. In fact, I think I should get the job in the next couple of years and not him. (Amy, no children)

Kate was different again. At the age of 38, she was married with two children. For a number of years she had developed a dual-focus career identity where career promotion had been accommodated to motherhood. However, her career identity was in the process of change. Having completed her mother-hood goals, she was now more consciously focusing on promotion in the career. Her career identity was shifting from a dual-focus career where promotion had been accommodated to a single-focus where promotion was antecedent.

Promotion was more of a problem before I had the children because there was always a question mark over me. I do remember when I had an interview for my job as Section Leader. One of the questions at that stage was 'When are you thinking of having a family?' or 'Are you thinking of having a family?' I had my family a year later but at that time I told them no, simply because I knew I wasn't going to get the job if I said I was.

Now having come back, the only problem I have is because of course I have an eight year gap and I have got a lot of catching up to do. I'm 38 and even though you could say that I'm in the fast lane in terms of where I've got to in a very short period of time, but my age is against me. At 38 I've got to make sure that I make at least one more move before I'm 40, and one shortly after I'm 40 to make some inroad into catching up.

My expectation of achievement has increased with every move I've made. Eventually by mid-40s my aim is to obtain a head of function position. That's the goal I have set myself and, if I obtain that, I suspect I shall want to do more! [laughter]. (Kate, two children)

These women in the careers history group whose career identity had a single focus and promotion was antecedent were strong-minded, forceful and deter-mined. A choice of appropriate descriptive words to use here is difficult since language itself is gendered (Coates, 1986). To describe women as assertive and determined has different connotations and conveys different images compared with using the same terms to describe men. These women were very ambitious. Three were already highly successful in promotional terms and the fourth was still at the start of her career. Two out of the four were single, although in stable partnerships. Three were childfree and the fourth had children at secondary school. For these women their work and careers currently ranked highest in their scale of priorities. Career development had been pursued or was now being pursued with single-minded determination. They had made and were making job moves in order to broaden their experience and enhance their CVs. They calculated the advantages and disadvantages of any jobs and assessed them in terms of their career and promotion potential. Their aspirations were to reach the top, or as far as possible, in career and promotion terms. Aspects of their personal lives were seen to support rather than to impinge or encroach on their work and professional responsibilities.

It was interesting to note that some of the men in the careers history group who were high achievers and who might be perceived as being in the single-focus, promotion antecedent category, were in fact becoming less single-focused in their career identities.

I can remember going on a training course when I was 27 or thereabouts, when I was asked that question [about career ambitions]. At that time I felt it was the right answer to say 'the sky's the limit'. That really wasn't an honest answer; it was what I thought I ought to say. Things change. In terms of remunerations, grading, I don't feel any strong ambitions in that respect any more. I think I require a job that is a challenge and is demanding. If it isn't that then I would get bored with the company . . . As to what's in front of me I've become fairly relaxed. I'm not ready yet for the carpet slippers, I will just see what comes. (Edward)

I think I am possibly in line for Head of Biology but the question I ask myself, I've been over it several times in the last few months, do I want to get further away from the science that I enjoy, into a position where I can influence things more. I don't know what the answer is to that question. (Nicholas)

I don't think I am as ambitious as some. There are clearly people around who are intent on empire-building and would climb over everybody they could to get to the Managing Director's chair. I don't see myself in that game. (Arthur)

It was interesting and somewhat ironic to note that as women were perhaps becoming more ambitious and more single-minded in their career ambitions, some men, who were already high-achievers, were becoming more calculating and more reluctant to devote themselves to a single-focus on promotion in their careers.

The dual-focus career: promotion accommodation

When career identity had a dual-focus, attempts were made to balance the personal and the work aspects of the self. When responsibilities conflicted and priority had to be allotted to one or other aspect, in this category priority was given to personal and family responsibilities. This meant that promotion in the career was held in abeyance while individuals worked to fulfil personal responsibilities. This could be perceived as a temporary situation, perhaps while children were small and until the individual could return to focus on promotion in their career. Alternatively, the accommodation of career to other aspects of self could be perceived as a longer-term or more permanent strategy for career identity. Certainly the consequences of promotion accommodation, for even a short period, were likely to continue to affect promotion achievements. The individual who opted out of career promotion for a period, perhaps developing a practitioner career (Crompton and Sanderson, 1990), was likely to achieve a lower promotion position overall. Traditionally this had been the career identity most commonly associated with women and for the women scientists and engineers in the careers history study, this was the most common career identity.

I think that if I had stayed without children and in full-time employment I would have gone several steps up the ladder by now, both from the interviews I had been offered and also the merit money I have been given. Over the past years I have been given considerable amounts of merit which again is an indication that they would like to keep you. (Anita, three children)

J.E.: Have you thought yet about what you're going to do when you've had the baby?
Carol: Yes. I intend to take full maternity leave, 29 weeks and then to return to work, which will be about August-time next year, but I feel very strongly that it should be on a reduced hours basis. I'm not prepared to go back full time. I've yet to battle that one out. I have given them full warning that I do intend to ask for reduced hours but it's the number of reduced hours that is still in question . . . I personally want a significant reduction because I want it for looking after my child. I want to be the primary carer, so I'd like to have four days at home and three days at work . . . we shall see! (Carol, about to have first baby)

We'd like another child so I think that limits me in my career. For instance I don't think I'd consider going for an interview for promotion while my first priority is my family. Certainly if we have another one I might consider part-time. When [my daughter] starts school I might ask for four weeks unpaid leave a year to help cover school holidays. There's no way if I was doing that that they would consider me for a [manager's] job. If I got promoted before that happened I wouldn't feel happy about it because you come under so much pressure at that level to do over-time, to be there when they need you, that I just couldn't do it. So I can't see me being promoted or wanting to be promoted for the next 5 years, maybe 10 years. If I have to wait 10 years, I'm 10 years older. I may lose some kind of enthusiasm and adaptability as I get older. They might be more inclined to go to someone else. If you have not applied for interview [for promotion] then you would be seen as not wanting to go on. (Miriam, one child)

For these women attempting a dual-focus career identity by accommodating promotion in the career, their aspirations were necessarily affected. They intended to wait and see. They were realistic, even resigned, to what this meant in promotion terms although some of them were reluctant to see promotion accommodation as a permanent resolution.

Although traditionally this pattern had been the typical woman's career identity, there was some evidence in the careers history group of husbands adopting the dual-focus, promotion accommodation pattern, at least for short periods.

When we first left university it was very easy to get teaching jobs but very difficult to get into industrial science. So that is why [my husband] followed me to Harlow. By the time I moved up here he was not working and I was not taking him away from any potential career down there. [He stayed home to care for the two children.] It was always at the back of our minds that he could teach up here. (Julie)

This was the only clear example of a husband adopting this career identity, however. Other husbands were prepared to negotiate over career moves and about alternative childcare arrangements, but resisted promotion accommodation for themselves. Indeed, it seemed as though the arrival of children acted as a spur to husbands' motivations for promotion since it frequently also entailed the slowing down, if not the actual stopping, of salary contributions from their wives.

The dual-focus career where promotion was accommodated to personal and family aspects of self was the most common career identity for the women scientists and engineers in the careers history group. They had modified their expectations for promotion and their aspirations for career were now centred on family and personal goals as well as on professional work. In the women's attempts to balance work and family commitments, some had negotiated a reduction in paid working hours and one woman was currently taking a career-break agreed and negotiated with the company. Promotion accommodation could be perceived as temporary or more permanent although the likely consequences for career and for subsequent promotion in the career were widely recognized. The women acknowledged the gender differences in the reconciling of private and public work responsibilities and for the most part accepted such differences. They were prepared, at least for the present, to negotiate a reduced paid work commitment in return for the satisfactions arising from family, motherhood and the feminine aspects of self. They were reconciled for the moment to the likely consequences of this for working careers and promotion possibilities, although they were unsure how they might feel about this eventually.

The dual-focus career: parenthood accommodation

When career identity had a dual focus it was also possible for personal and family aspirations to be accommodated in order to develop the career. In this case it was parenthood which was either not possible or was postponed in order to enable career and promotion ambitions to be prioritized. When career identity involved the accommodation of parenthood goals this was regarded as either a permanent solution to the management of career and personal responsibilities (probably through an inability to have children) or as a more short-term interim measure. When parenthood was accommodated in a dual-focus career identity, either through an inability to have children or through their postponement, then aspirations for career and promotion achievements were likely to be very high. At the time of the careers history interviews, 13 women and five of the men were without children. For some of these this was a positive choice to enable a single-focus on promotion in the career. For others, however, this was less of a positive choice; their career identities still had a dual focus but parenthood was not possible.

> At my last interview [within Marlands] I was asked when was I starting a family . . . I said 'Well I don't appear to be able to have any children', and he was so embarrassed he apologised . . . I'm not a total career person. It has to be a balance; my home life is more important to me than a high-powered career. I enjoy running the house; I enjoy gardening; I enjoy cooking. Also, I'm extremely proud of what [my husband's] done and I like to think that some of that is because he's had, well I hope, a happy home life, and that I've been able to remove some of the worries like paying the bills, doing the

cleaning, the housework, everyday things. He can come in and work until midnight every night, which is what he has done for quite a long time. (Sylvia)

For respondents like Sylvia, their career identities were still dual-focused but in her case, of necessity, parenthood had been accommodated. Her husband had been extremely successful in promotion terms (he was not a respondent in the careers history group) and she had also been promotion-successful to a process manager position in Marlands.

For others in this category, parenthood had been postponed, initially as an interim measure, in an attempt to solve the management of career and personal responsibilities.

Do I really want children? Do I actually want to have a family? I think really when I come down to it, the answer is probably no. I mean there is a lot of 'yes' within that, in terms of not having a family means that you do miss out on an awful lot, but the other aspect is what would you give up to actually do that? Not just in terms of work, but yourself, your relationship with your partner, your own hobbies, what you want to do. To some extent that has got an impact back to childhood. I was from quite a large family and my mother was very ill, from when I was about 11, so a lot of the bringing up the younger children, I did the majority of that. Although I know that there would be an awful lot that I would miss out on, there is also a lot I would gain by not having them. I like doing a lot of other things, in terms of travelling, in terms of holidaying, I fly light aircrafts – all those sorts of things that need a lot of time and effort. I know that if I had children, they would almost all have to go totally. If I do the balance and it is not 100% [laughter] I've still got a couple of years. But I'd be surprised if I had them now . . . I mean if I had to put some guesstimates down now as to what would my career look like, what would I do, I guess probably within about a year or so, I'll be doing a different job. It'll be a promotion because I have done three sideways moves to gain experience in different things. Which again if I had to guess probably wouldn't be back with Materials, it would be something different like Development and maybe do that for 3, 4 years or so, and then get a Company Senior Staff job in one of the related fields. And then from that . . . (Vivian, no children)

When career identity was dual-focused and parenthood was accommodated, the achievements and aspirations for promotion in the career were likely to be very high. This was also the case for the men in the careers history study who were childfree, because of postponement or an inability to have children, and whose careers retained a dual-focus on partnerships, wider family, voluntary, sport and leisure activities in addition to career.

The single-focus career: parenthood antecedence

Career identity could also have a single focus where parenthood was anteced-ent. This category is included for analytical completeness. No one in the careers history group could be described as having this career identity, since such an identity involved giving up the career either temporarily or longer term in order to concentrate exclusively on caring responsibilities. All the women and men in the careers history group except one had paid work positions in Airmax or Marlands at the time of the interview. The one excep-tion was Anita who was taking a career break. However, Anita still maintained contact with the company and had a date for her return to her career after the break; she maintained contact with her work and her department. For these reasons Anita's identity was more appropriately described as dual rather than single-focus with promotion accommodation. As the careers history study was about women and men currently in working careers, the experiences of women and men giving precedence to parenthood could not be examined. Clearly, giving up careers for a period in order to concentrate on parenthood is still a common career strategy for many women although there are sugges-tions that such a strategy occupies fewer (particularly professional) women and for shorter periods of time (McRae, 1991). There was also one woman in the careers history study whose husband had temporarily given up *his* career for full-time parenting.

For women there are clear links between single-focus parenthood ident-ities and dual-focus promotion accommodation identities. Probably a majority of women of child-bearing age at any one time will be in one or other of these two categories or be moving from one identity to the other. In the single-focus parenthood identity, the self is perceived primarily in terms of parenthood (motherhood) rather than paid work. This might be a short- or a long-term identity. When career identities are focused on parenthood, individuals at that time will be taking time out of their paid work careers in order to fulfil family responsibilities. Also, and increasingly, family obligations are not confined to childcare. Adult children, women for the most part, undertake the responsi-bilities associated with the care of elderly relatives.

Traditionally this has been a career identity associated primarily with women. Women whose careers are focused on family concerns will take time out of their paid-work careers while their children are young. They might return to part-time or full-time work when family responsibilities ease but their family roles as wife, mother and carer are most important to their sense of self. They perceive themselves as wives and mothers first and as paid workers only in so far as this does not affect their primary identities. Alterna-tively such women might never return to paid work or might alter their paid work to better suit their family responsibilities.

When careers are focused on parenthood, women will be unambitious for promotion in their paid work. Either they do not seek or they consciously reject promotion in the career. For women with this career identity their self-image is primarily as wives and mothers and this is the greatest source of satisfaction and identity. For many years such a career identity fitted conventional norms of socially acceptable behaviour; these women put their personal commitments to husbands, children (and parents) first.

Later in the career when family commitments ease and husbands become less mobile and more stable in respect of their own careers, the identities of some women in this category might alter. The most likely change is a move from a single-focus, motherhood antecedent identity to a dual-focus, promotion accommodation career. In such cases promotion in the career might have to be accommodated either because the paid work has no promotion or career positions or because, even if there are promotion positions, the reality of hierarchical career structures requires continuous regular progression or little progression at all. However, many women are nevertheless reconciled to such a dual-focus where through a balance between paid and unpaid work, they derive satisfaction from their dual-focused career identities.

Traditionally, this category has probably been the preserve of women since they have most often left their jobs to care for babies and children. Women have also predominated in occupations without career structures. Similarly for women in careered occupations either they have not sought or have not achieved promotion in the career. However, conditions are changing. A (very) few men are adopting this career identity at least for short periods. In addition, the large majority of women now undertake paid work for a substantial proportion of their adult lives. It is likely, therefore, that the single-focus career where parenthood is antecedent is now only a short-term career identity and one whose numerical significance in general is declining. However, the consequences for women (and men) of adopting this identity, even for a short period of time, will continue to affect and influence career outcomes.

Conclusion

The women and men scientists and engineers in the careers history study had developed different career identities. This chapter has examined the different ways in which individuals negotiate and reconcile domestic, professional and career identities in the course of their working lives. It has explored the notion of career identity as the individual's perception of self in respect of promotion and achievement in the career positions and hierarchies of work organizations. In attempting to reconcile professional scientific and engineering work with personal and cultural identities, these women and men had become workers of a particular kind, with different attitudes to and aspirations for their careers. They had balanced the personal and public aspects of their lives in different ways; they had different priorities in respect of career and personal goals.

The large majority of respondents in the careers history study were in dual-career partnerships where both adult partners were in professional occupations with clear opportunities for and expectations of promotion and career development. In research, the incidence of dual-career couples has often been exaggerated. The preponderance of women in routine white-collar work meant that husbands might be developing careers while their wives were in jobs with no formal career or promotion ladders. Also, even where both partners were in jobs with careers, there had been a marked tendency for the man's career interests to take priority over those of the woman. Alternatively, men have been able to develop what Acker (1980) called 'two-person careers' where non-working wives supported their husbands' careers and took on responsibility for domestic and caring duties.

The responses of the women in the careers history study, though admittedly an élite group, indicated that for them such conditions have to change and indeed were already changing. The men were increasingly having to take account of their partners' career interests in deciding their own. The necessity for dual-career negotiation rather than single-career commitment was putting limitations on men's career moves. The need to balance career developments between partners was becoming more critical if the partnership was to continue.

New patterns of domestic arrangements were also emerging. Some of the careers history respondents were making arrangements for paid childcare rather than taking career breaks or developing practitioner careers. Others had mentioned 'weekend marriages' where partners lived and worked apart during the week and came together only at weekends. None of the careers history respondents were involved in such arrangements, though several claimed knowledge of couples in such domestic patterns.

Difficulties continue and must not be underestimated. The lack of childcare, and care for the elderly, facilities which are perceived as appropriate cause practical problems as well as career difficulties, particularly for women although difficulties are not confined to them. It is also necessary to acknowledge that in respect of career achievements and promotion success, men have more cultural and ideological support. The high-achieving man wins admiration and respect; the high-achieving woman is perceived as lacking in essential aspects of femininity, caring and relatedness. These continuing differences in cultural attributes and expectations pose career difficulties and dilemmas for women.

This chapter has suggested four alternative types of career identity and suggested there is frequent movement between the types over the course of career histories. In focusing on identity, career has been made an individual rather than a collective or household process. This decision was deliberate. It would have been possible to examine household or partnership decisions about careers. It was felt, however, that where researchers *had* focused on household decision-making rather than individual decisions, there was a danger that the power processes behind the household decision might remain unexplored (Crow, 1989). It might, for example, have worked to disguise some of the resource differences which men and women have in attempting to manage their public and private lives. Men have ideological support and confirmation for career development and progress whereas women developing careers are path-finders in an, as yet, relatively unsympathetic and underresourced world.

Chapter 7

Promotion in the Career: Organizational Constraints and Personal Resolutions

In recent years there has been growing interest in the ways in which organizational processes interrelate and interact and how such processes operate to define the realities of everyday working lives. This is particularly the case with promotion in the career. The promotion structures or ladders which are developed within industrial and other organizations are objectified in the experiences and perceptions of individuals. Promotion comes to be perceived as a matter of acquiring the stated criteria and necessary experience needed for the next position. For higher-grade promotion posts, the criteria are usually less clear, unwritten and more subjective – more a matter of networking, self-presentation and an element of luck. These perceptions, however, define the limits to as well as the opportunities for careers. In this way they constitute constraints on the possible; and the constraints are structural as well as cultural.

It is important again to emphasize, however, that developing a career is not only a process of adaptation. The individual is an active agent and this means purposive choices and actions following them and implies a 'productive processor of reality' (Hurrelmann, 1988). The *consequences* of certain choices might be a reproduction of organizational structures and processes and of particular individual perceptions of promotion 'success' or 'failure'. It is necessary, nevertheless, to consider the ways in which women and men are active in managing rather than merely passively adapting to cultural expectations and structural constraints in their professional careers.

Gender constitutes a critical variable in the way organizational structures and processes are reproduced in organizations. Savage and Witz (Eds, 1992) have reviewed the theoretical developments which have resulted in gender and organizations having a prominent place in contemporary social theory. From the early focus on bureaucratic organization, feminists have moved the discussion to how those bureaucracies are gendered. This has included feminist theories of the State as well as analysis of organizational sexuality and Savage and Witz see shortcomings in these lines of development. Instead they argue for a return to the organizational and bureaucratic focus and how this relates to gender processes and gender relations. 'The centrepiece of this perspective is the relationship between gender and power within organizational settings' (Savage and Witz, 1992, p. 56), what they term the 'gender paradigm' for the study of organizations.

The discussion in this chapter will attempt an analysis of the 'gender paradigm' in the promotion experiences of the careers history respondents in the two industrial organizations of Airmax and Marlands. The focus will be the women and men engineers and scientists and how their career actions and behaviour contribute to gendered processes within the organizations. First, the structural aspects of promotion in the two organizations will be considered. This will be followed by an examination of the cultural influences on promotion. Then the responses and personal resolutions of the careers history women and men who were actively constructing and developing their careers will be analysed. An assessment will be made of how individual actions resulted in specific types of gender configuration. The processes of gender in the organization pose difficulties for men who are ambivalent in respect of promotion. Similarly, gendered processes pose numerous paradoxes for women who are striving to get outside the accepted and acceptable positions of secretary and personal assistant. 'At the same time, they must behave like men and yet be women. This is the paradox of women's organizational experiences' (Savage and Witz, 1992, p. 53).

Structural aspects of promotion

Research on careers in the 1950s and 1960s focused on organizational career structures and ladders and, as a result, the notions of progress and promotion came to be attached to the concept of career. Later research, particularly in the interactionist tradition, extended the concept beyond paid work so that wives (Finch, 1983), deviants (Becker, 1963), psychiatric patients (Goffman, 1968) and prisoners (Taylor and Cohen, 1972) were also considered as having careers. However, for careers in paid work, the notion of progress within organizations and professions, in regular and successive stages, and of movement into jobs with increasing responsibility came to be attached to the term career (Wilensky, 1960; Slocum, 1966). In paid work, careers could best be pursued where there were hierarchically arranged promotion positions, usually in bureaucratic organizational structures, through which position-holders were able to move in regular and successive stages, achieving promotion to more responsible and more highly paid posts.

It is necessary to remember, however, that promotion in organizations and professions usually requires individuals to do less professional work and more management of others who are doing the professional work: promotion and career development increasingly involve moving into management. The different effects of this for the science and engineering respondents in the careers history study were considered in Chapter 5.

The women and men engineers in the careers history group were working for an organization which had confronted the issue of engineering-management career progression. Trade unions in the organization had eventually persuaded the company to agree to set up (among other things) a parallel professional ladder to run alongside the managerial ladder. This had enabled some individuals in the company to progress in career terms by developing professional specialist skills rather than managerial expertise. This new promotion structure had not been operating for very long but there was already some cynicism among the engineers about the effects of such a system. The engineers had doubts about how difficult it was to progress up the professional ladder and in respect of it being a dead-end in career terms. It was widely understood to be the case that only management posts could lead to the highest positions in the company.

For the graduate engineers at Airmax, the ways to achieve promotion at the lower levels on the technologists scale were known, the criteria were understood and were widely accepted. There were four promotion levels with a minimum wait at each level of two years. The criteria for promotion to the next level were clearly specified and individuals who were able to fulfil such criteria, and who had the support of their managers, could apply for promotion to the next level. Such a structure would enable both women and men at Airmax to pursue the stated promotion criteria and operationalize a 'qualifications lever' (Crompton and Sanderson, 1990) in their search for promotion. Beyond the technologists scale, the promotion structure divided into a professional/technical ladder and a managerial ladder, each with three levels. Promotion on the professional ladder continued to be clearly specified and depended on work done. In that sense promotion was retrospective: individuals had to demonstrate they had operated at a particular level before getting promoted to it. In theory there were no number limits although it was recognized that the company would not permit too many, high-cost professional people to be appointed. The managerial ladder was more traditional, however. Here promotion depended on vacancies and the needs of the company. Management potential was less clearly specified, there was no minimum wait at each level and indeed it was possible to leapfrog and to miss levels should the company require it. This was also the case with the next set of promotion positions, the company senior staff. Here there was no system of application; as with management positions, these posts were by invitation only. It was widely assumed that only management positions could lead to senior staff posts and at this level, in any case, numbers were very small and exclusive.

For the graduate scientists and programmers at Marlands, the promotion ladders were more variable. There were equivalent, standardized, early-promotion positions (scientist, senior scientist, principal scientist; programmer, analyst programmer, senior analyst programmer) where promotion was more or less automatic and regular assuming satisfactory performance. The senior positions here could involve managerial responsibilities but the next step, team leader, was the first recognized position on the complex managerial ladder. Further positions, such as section/project leader, senior section leader culminated in senior management posts such as head of section/department/ process positions.

These then were the structural aspects of career and promotion in Airmax and Marlands. For the women and men in the careers history study, these formed the contexts within which promotion could be pursued and careers developed. These ladders constituted the objective constructs by means of which careers could be built. However, these structural aspects were likely to affect the promotion achievements of the women in a different way to the men.

The promotion achievements of women in organizations and in the professions have been a growing theme in the research literature (Hearn *et al.*, Eds, 1989; Atkinson and Delamont, 1990; Davidson and Cooper, 1992; Evetts, 1994a). There is a considerable body of evidence that women are excluded from access to professional and organizational career ladders (Kanter, 1977; Collinson and Knights, 1986; Crompton and Sanderson, 1990). One way they are excluded is through gender differentiated recruitment whereby men and women train and apply for different jobs (Savage, 1992b). In this way occupational segregation is perpetuated through structural as well as ideological means. There are other mechanisms, however, and these have been receiving increased attention in recent years as more women have been training for and recruited on to the bottom levels of career ladders. The processes of organizational sexuality (Hearn *et al.*, Eds, 1989) and of social closure (Witz, 1990, 1992) have all been used to explain the lower promotion achievements of women.

Before the promotion positions of the women and men in the careers history group are summarized, it must be remembered that the careers history respondents had been selected as far as possible to represent all the promotion positions in Airmax and Marlands. In addition, there were 31 women in the careers history group and only 10 men. So these summary numbers cannot be used to demonstrate gender differences in promotion achievements. Certain aspects of their promotion progress were becoming apparent, however, and might be regarded as indicative of emerging gendered patterns in engineering and science careers.

Of the 15 women and five men engineers working for Airmax, nine women and two men were on the technologists scale; three were in professional positions (two women, one man); four were in managerial posts (three women, one man); one man was company senior staff and one woman was a director.

Of the 16 women and five men scientists and programmers working for Marlands, six women and no men were in the early career positions (scientist, programmer); nine were in middle-management positions of team leader to senior section/project leader (five women, four men); two (one women, one man) were in senior management posts. This left four women who were in management posts which were difficult to categorize. This was because of the complexity of the management hierarchy in this company and also because of organizational restructuring and development, which will be examined in Chapter 9.

These, then, were the promotion positions in the two organizations of the women and men in the careers history study. Clearly, promotion required certain characteristics and the promotion-successful were required to demonstrate those characteristics in order to succeed. Some of the characteristics were job-specific and the skills were necessitated by the particular position. There were also certain general characteristics associated with the promotion-successful and some of these were cultural requirements.

Cultural influences on promotion

The cultural aspects of promotion, the beliefs and attitudes associated with promotion achievement, include the images (as well as the symbols) that are associated with career success as well as the expectations that attach to promotion achievement. The images associated with career success are ability, hard work, determination and competition. These characteristics are mostly gender-neutral and could be associated with promotion-successful women and men. These characteristics also coincide with the meritocratic image most organizations would wish to promote: that individuals are promoted through their personal achievements, attitudes and attributes.

Other images are less gender-neutral, however. Promotion success also implies being strong and decisive, standing out, being pushy, getting oneself noticed. A strong element of likeness and similarity is also implicit, as when senior managers choose to sponsor and promote those most like themselves. These images, however, have very different connotations when they are associated with a woman than when associated with a man. The strong, decisive, pushy man is admired while a similar woman is likely to be perceived as aggressive, domineering and bitchy. It is similarly difficult for women to be chosen for sponsorship because of likeness or commonality. Gender difference remains a fundamental barrier, therefore, even when attitudes, achievements and other background factors are held in common.

The symbols of promotion success are also an aspect of competition in the organization. The separate office, the personal secretary, the company car, even the carpet and the name plate can be perceived, even promoted, as symbols of achievement. Such symbols might even be used in organizations to motivate employees as an alternative to monetary or promotion rewards. Such symbols have been male preserves in the past although they are becoming gender-neutral as they are competed for by both women and men in organizations.

The expectations that attach to promotion success are closely related to the images already considered. Expectations can be self-imposed and they can be reflections of models of work patterns of seniors as well as a way of establishing differences and distinctiveness from juniors. Thus the promotion-successful are expected to put in long working hours, to arrive early and to leave late. Holiday entitlements are seldom fully used and some will be postponed or cancelled should the work needs of the organization require it. Other expectations might include a willingness to relocate, to stand in for a senior colleague, never to be ill or to have family responsibilities. The ability to meet such expectations is clearly gender differentiated. As long as the family is perceived to be primarily the responsibility of women, men will be able to match up to such expectations much more easily than women. Women who choose to stay single or childfree, however, might well be able, even willing, to meet such requirements. Also, it is necessary to remember that many men might be unwilling.

In general, however, men are not perceived as experiencing contradictions between their gender and promotion ambitions and expectations. It is entirely appropriate for men to work hard and to put in long hours in their organizations where women would be perceived as neglectful of their personal and family responsibilities. Sheppard's women managers (1989) perceived themselves and other women to be constantly confronting the dualistic experience of being 'feminine' and 'businesslike' at the same time. 'Learning how to manage the world of organization necessarily implies learning how to redefine and manage "femaleness"'(Sheppard, 1989, p. 144). The growing presence of women in what have traditionally been male positions has heightened awareness of these contradictions. At the same time, feminist scholarship has revealed the prevalence of male experience, how that interpretation is normative and how it excludes much of women's experience.

Personal resolutions

The question is, then, how were the women and men in the careers history group dealing with the expectations for promotion in the career? How were they managing the cultural and structural constraints and opportunities offered by their organizations? Were there any fundamental differences between the resolutions of the women and the men in the careers history group? Where there were differences, were these resulting in particular types of gender configuration within the organizations? Two different kinds of resolution will be explored: the first were decisions or circumstances in respect of having children; the second were decisions in respect of career moves within the organization.

Decisions in respect of parenthood

The decision to marry or to have a permanent relationship is now less critical in respect of the impact on promotion and career. Marriage and partnerships continue to have some effect, however. For both partners, career moves must now be negotiated and balanced, particularly in dual-career families. This might well result in decisions being made for other than career and promotion reasons. Much of the research literature continues to assert that the man's career and promotion continue to take priority in family and partnership decision-making. This was not always the case for the respondents in the careers history group, however, and it was definitely not the case for the women scientists in that group. The extent of change in this respect must await further research.

The decision to become parents is probably now the most significant in its effect on careers and promotion. Parenthood presents a particular set of expectations and responsibilities. Children have to be cared for at all times by one or other parent or both, or alternative care arrangements have to be made. There are also particular kinds of expectations about what is 'appropriate' care. Such expectations and responsibilities pose dilemmas for all parents but particularly for those in dual-career families.

Choosing to be, or of necessity remaining, childfree
The decision to remain childfree or the discovery of an inability to have children is one obvious way out of the dilemmas which parenthood poses, particularly for promotion in the career. The decision to remain childfree is clearly a very different circumstance from an inability to have children but the consequences might be similar. Both partners might focus on promotion and career as an alternative. Thompson, Thomas and Maier (1992) have suggested that career women are developing different resolutions to the family/career dilemmas compared with career men. They suggest that whereas career men might currently be experiencing higher levels of conflict over career and family expectations, some career women might be anticipating such conflicts and resolving them by avoiding parenthood. It might be the case, therefore, that in choosing the childfree state, these are particular kinds of couple in career terms. In choosing to focus on their careers, it is likely such couples would be highly ambitious and possibly also very successful in promotion terms.

This was generally the case with the women and men in the careers history group who had chosen to remain childfree. Most were career-ambitious and also promotion-successful. For the majority, the decision to remain childfree was unambiguous.

I'm a career woman. I don't intend to have any family. I'm in a situation where I do live with somebody, both of us for our own reasons don't want children. We are quite happy with the set-up that we've got and I'm not very maternal. I quite like children but I don't want any of my own. I actually do want a career. (Beryl)

For others the decision was not quite as clear-cut.

Do I really want children? Do I actually want to have a family? I think really when I come down to it, the answer is probably 'no'. I mean there is a lot of 'yes' within that, in terms of not having a family means that you do miss out on an awful lot . . . (Vivian)

In terms of having a family myself, we have decided not to have children ourselves but in a few years I am quite seriously thinking of actually trying to adopt older children, maybe six or seven years, and we are not bothered about adopting children with any sort of physical disabilities. (Susan)

The decision to remain childfree and instead to focus on promotion achievements at work is one way of resolving the dilemmas which parenthood presents, particularly for women. This is a harsh decision for some women, however, and career men are not faced with the same dilemma unless they are in dual-career partnerships. Nevertheless it seems that for both women and men to succeed in promotion, they must severely curtail the demands of personal and family lives. The organization is more likely to reward single-minded dedication to its work with promotion in the career.

Combining career and parenthood

For the women and men in the careers history group who were parents, arrangements about childcare were a daily feature of their working lives. Fathers sometimes assisted, most often in sharing responsibility for taking children to schools or to childminders. However, the responsibilities for collecting children, taking time off work for children who were sick and making arrangements to cover school holidays, remained with the mothers. In general, the outcome of negotiations over childcare within families was for the women to continue to be the prime carers. The exceptions to this pattern were few (e.g. Julie) and usually for limited periods of time.

In order to fit childcare in with a developing career, for some, negotiations also had to take place with managers in their work organizations. Such negotiations were confined to the women respondents, however. The fathers rarely, if ever, entered into such negotiations with their own managers. Fathers preferred to take holiday rather than negotiating to leave early or arrive late. For several of the women respondents, however, such negotiations were entered into and compromises were eventually agreed. The women were required to negotiate as individuals and the attitudes and powers of particular managers continued to be the deciding factor. Some of the women had been the first, or perceived themselves to be the first, in their organizations to negotiate particular working arrangements.

Because my husband works at the company and because he talked to people in the area that I used to work in, in 1974, he said they're recruiting again, why don't you see if you can go back for just part-time. It was just unheard of (at Airmax) in those days, but one of the managers that my husband had a lift-share with, talked to my previous manager and he agreed he would be happy to consider it. But it took about six months to get it argued through the Personnel Department and, I am told, it went through to Director level and everyone threw up their hands – 'Part-time, this is terrible'. But it worked out and they agreed to take me. A lot of senior managers were unhappy about it at the time. I think it depended on partly the Personnel Department accepting that their system could cope with a part-timer. They were thinking of the computer systems, and the pay-roll and all the other work booking systems, and also the manager of the Department and whether he was prepared to take someone part-time. I know a couple of managers said they would not consider it – but one manager did. (Ann)

I don't need full-time care anymore but I do need full-time care in the holidays. I went to Marlands and asked if I could have an extra five weeks unpaid leave a year so that I could take time off in the school holidays, and rather to my surprise they agreed. (Jennifer)

The current arrangement I am on at the moment is reduced hours in the sense that I work 32½ hours instead of 37½ hours. Basically, my hours are 8.35 am until 3.15 pm ... At that time there was nothing else on offer from [Airmax]. Now they have actually brought out other guidelines that you can have career breaks and come back part-time, whereas when I negotiated my terms, there was maybe one or two other women who had actually broached that subject and it was very much left to the discretion of your manager and the value of your job to what terms you got. (Pat)

There is a career break scheme which is operated informally. An individual negotiates with her manager. It very much depends on the relationship you have with your immediate manager. But there is an effort there and if what they are offering matches you, and the climate of your local management matches your desires at the time, but it's not going to satisfy everyone's desires and situations. (Mary)

These women perceived themselves to be negotiating with their organizations as individuals. They had to justify their worth and the value to the companies from agreeing to the arrangements. The decision of particular managers was the critical factor: their managers had to agree to the resolution. In addition, the requirements of particular posts and positions rendered them inaccessible for such arrangements: there were certain no-go areas for women with children who wanted a reduced time commitment for a period.

Marlands have recently introduced a career break scheme which is for all members of staff. In your working lifetime you can have up to five years as a career break. But it is perceived as being most unlikely that anybody at the forefront of the science area is going to be able to use that. On the basis that within six months you can be out of touch with the current science because it is such a fast moving area. (Pauline)

If you are going to have a career break or part-time, you've really got to get yourself into the right sort of circumstances, where it can still be in the company's interest to keep you on. You've still got to have something to offer them so that it's an economic decision. You're never going to get a company to enjoy keeping people on just because they are told to. (Alice)

The only difficulty I see in my position is the fact we're a manufacturing area and I do feel for the company; part-time working, flexible working, may cause problems because you've got the pressure of getting the components out. I do work very closely with a colleague in terms of what's on the shop floor but you can't always just switch off at 2.30 or 12 o'clock and say right this is your job now because you can't just hand over something half way through. And [there is] the shift pattern of course in the manufacturing area. I don't think it is simple because you are not just working on your own projects all the time. You've got to consider if you are looking at it, the company is obviously looking from their point of view, that is the way the company works. (Elizabeth)

It seems then that both the men and the women in the careers history group were active, not just passively adapting in combining career and parenthood in their industrial organizations. For the most part, the men had prioritized their work. Occasionally, when childcare presented dilemmas which only fathers could resolve, they took holiday entitlements which avoided pleading family responsibilities. The only childcare task they appreciably shared was the delivery of children to schools, nurseries and childminders and this could usually be done without arriving late to work.

The women were also very active in developing solutions to the dilemmas which parenthood presented to careers in their organizations. Their solutions attempted a balance, which was perceived differently by each woman. The resolutions were individually negotiated and represented personal compromises to the career/parenthood dilemmas. The women's solutions were also in sympathy with, not in opposition to, their organization's demands. The women conceded the necessity of the companies' requirements. The needs of the organizations, for full-time work commitments and no family responsibilities, were perceived as commonsense; such reasoning was presented and accepted as rational. The women were developing individualized and personalized resolutions which were in correspondence with the needs of the organizations and not in opposition to them.

Decisions within the organization

In addition to alternative arrangements in respect of parenthood and childcare, there was also some scope for different career promotion developments with Airmax and Marlands. There was not just *one* career ladder but several and the consequences of particular moves were not always apparent. Career moves were also presented as conscious decisions though clearly some were necessitated, for example, by a company reorganization.

Avoiding management and building a reputation

For some in the careers history group, their careers had involved promotion on a professional ladder rather than a move into management. This was easier to detect in respect of the engineers, where Airmax had a professional promotion ladder in addition to its managerial hierarchy. At Marlands the promotion ladder was a common one, but where a position was a technically specialist post with no managerial responsibilities for others, this was assumed to be synonymous with a professional position.

Both women and men were in professional positions. For some this was a conscious choice to enable the individual to continue to develop a specialist area of expertise. This was of particular interest to some of the Marlands scientists, for example. For others, and in this case the women, a professional post was a conscious decision to facilitate career development in the organization.

I've gone for the professional specialist route. I was fortunate in being able to match the criteria. I've given papers at specialist defraction conferences. I've also jointly written and published papers, spin-offs from working in my area. I've got international recognition, I think I can say that ... I've grown myself into a niche. Perhaps it might be dangerous in terms of career, but it's an area I enjoy. (Mary, principal technologist)

If you want a family, you are much better going up the professional ladder because you can't really manage a department on reduced hours. You've got to put in all your hours and some more. For most people who would prefer not to, they tend to go up the professional ladder. (Alice, company specialist)

It's very difficult to pinpoint if you are suffering from any discrimination. There have been in the past, several times when I have gone for man management jobs and I haven't had them, even though people around me said they were surprised I didn't get them. But, Senior Management has always managed to come up with a reasonable explanation as to why I didn't get it, that's maybe quite valid. Whether it has anything to do with the fact that I am female, I don't know. But the women that I know of, the majority of them are on the professional ladder. (Carol, professional technologist)

There are ways of doing what I have done which is find yourself a nice position and become an expert and be paid for that expertise. There are ways with the sort of salary structure which Marlands uses which allows payment for expertise. (Sarah Jane, technical information officer)

If choosing the professional route and avoiding management, or being persuaded out of management, was one possible solution for reducing the dilemmas posed by career, the problem of achieving promotion in the organization still had to be solved. For the women in the careers history group the answer was merit: apparently simple even though difficult to achieve in practice. Airmax and Marlands had successfully promoted themselves as meritocratic organizations. The solution was to build a reputation, to get oneself known as competent, regardless of gender. The answer was in the hands of individual women: the need was to be *good* at the job.

In general, then, avoiding management or being persuaded into other kinds of posts and developing a professional specialist career was one way of achieving promotion as well as accommodating private and personal responsibilities and, in addition, pursuing a particular kind of occupational identity. Promotion and career in organizations was dependent on merit; building a reputation was a viable objective for both women and men.

The career routes of the promotion-successful
An examination of the promotion routes and moves of the four most successful women and men in the careers history group demonstrated the uses that *could* be made of promotion ladders by the promotion-ambitious. Frances had joined Airmax in 1975 immediately after graduating in production engineering. She had moved positions five times in the next 11 years both for promotion and to extend her experience. Then she was head-hunted and for the next three years she left Airmax and worked for another smaller company; and after the first year she was promoted to managing director. Finally she was head-hunted again, this time by Airmax and she returned to a director post. Francis was unmarried although in a stable partnership and she was childfree.

Edward had joined Airmax after graduating in economics and materials in 1980. In the next nine years he had achieved six promotions, at least three of which were a result of reorganizations. He had always worked for Airmax. He was married; his wife was developing a career in banking and he had a small son.

Sylvia graduated with a degree in chemistry in 1974 and she completed her PhD in 1977. She worked for another company and after two years moved to Marlands. In the next 10 years she had moved posts four times within

Marlands and had also achieved promotions within those posts. She was seriously considering moving to another company in order to add to her experience and promotion prospects. Sylvia was married to a career-successful engineer and they had no children.

Finally, Arthur had joined Marlands immediately after completing his PhD in 1975; his first degree was in maths, computing and statistics. He had joined the operations research team and had achieved regular and systematic promotions over the next 15-year period to his current post as senior systems manager. Arthur's career was spent wholly at Marlands. He was married to a civil servant and they had no children.

The patterns of these four promotion-successful careers displayed similarities. All four had made frequent, regular and systematic moves. Most moves had been accompanied by promotion but moves to widen and extend their experience or to change to a different area were also common. Company reorganizations and making good use of such changes were also common in the four careers. It also seemed to be important from the four accounts to 'let it be known' particularly to immediate and other managers that a move was desired. Career contentment and satisfaction were not exactly a handicap – Frances had greatly enjoyed every post – but a degree of restlessness, of looking forward and of forward planning seemed to be important.

In the research and feminist literature, these patterns are usually per-ceived as being more difficult for women to match than for men. There is no doubt that this is the case, particularly for women with husbands' careers and with children to manage. Frances and Sylvia *had* developed such patterns of regular and systematic movement and progress in their careers and neither women had children. Also, it was interesting to note that Frances and Sylvia had both spent periods of time in other companies in the development of their careers whereas both Edward and Arthur had stayed in the same company. Further investigation would be necessary but perhaps successful women have to more than match, in fact have to exceed, the 'normal' male pattern in order to reach the highest levels of promotion-achievement.

The managerial women

What of the careers history women who had achieved managerial positions in their organizations? Some of the issues in respect of gender and management are examined in Chapter 8 and the details of the respondents' experiences are postponed until then. The managerial women were all very interesting case-studies and their personal circumstances as well as particular experiences were variable. Through their accounts of their careers, it was possible to become aware of the requirements laid down by their work organizations for pro-motion into managerial posts.

In general, hard work, long hours and a single-minded dedication to the efficiency and productivity of the work team was a first requirement. In such posts, women managers were the intermediaries between the higher level decision-makers and planners (usually men) and the section members who were doing the scientific and engineering work (could be mostly women, mostly men or a mix of both). They were required to operationalize decisions, effect changes in work practices and job responsibilities, explain the need for changes and defend them, while at the same time persuading the reluctant and encouraging the ambitious members of their teams. Women who were not prepared for a single-minded focus on the needs of the organization would be ill-equipped for such positions.

> It's either you give up a partnership, family or you give up things that you enjoy doing outside of work. Because I don't believe that there's any way you would get to a senior position without putting in more than thirty-seven hours a week. If I look at what I am doing now, I never leave work before about half past six, sometimes it's later than that. Do I really have to have that continue? You see some of the chiefs there, they are in Saturdays and Sundays, they hardly take any holidays. You do question what is it all for, unless you are getting such a kick out of it, that it totally over-rides everything else in your life. If it does, that is fine, if that's what you want to do in your life. (Vivian)

There were also some other requirements. There were aspects of self-presentation and perception which required the women to walk a tightrope in their attempts to reconcile being efficient with being women. The women needed to be decisive; the alternative was to be weak; but they risked being perceived as overbearing. They needed to be assertive; the alternative was to be feeble, though they risked being perceived as aggressive. They needed to be competitive; the alternative was to be passive, but they risked being perceived as belligerent. These were the dilemmas which the contradictory demands of being women and being managers required. The experiences of the careers history women managers confirmed the findings of Sheppard (1989) when she described the strategies which women managers are required to employ in order to blend into the organization. Such a blending depended on very careful management of being feminine enough (in terms of appearance, self-presentation, acceptance of different expectations and of caring responsibilities) while at the same time being businesslike enough (competent, desiring promotion to a point and in particular directions) in order to claim a rightful place in the organization.

From promotion experiences to gendered processes

This chapter has examined the structural and cultural aspects of promotion in two organizations, together with the responses and personal resolutions of the respondents in the careers history group. It remains to consider whether the different responses of the women and men scientists and engineers were resulting in particular types of gender configuration within the organizations.

In general, promotion in the career is problematic for women. It is more problematic for women than for men in organizations because for a long time men have monopolized particularly the higher-level promotion positions. It is also more problematic for women since in science and engineering careers in organizations, promotion involves moving into managerial posts. Both women and men are reluctant to be managed by a woman. In the careers history group, some women had avoided such difficulties by developing professional, technical-specialist careers. Savage (1992a) has argued that such career positions are rapidly becoming a more general feature of organizational and managerial change and that the gendered aspects of such changes are important. For the women scientists and engineers, this type of career enabled them to overcome both the cultural difficulties of management as well as the structural constraints of full-time, long hours and extensive work commitments. Such positions could also enable the women to balance the public and private aspects of their careers.

Some of the difficulties of science and engineering management for women could be coped with by giving precedence to promotion and career in the organization. The careers of the women who were already managers demonstrated the sorts of requirements which the organization demanded, as well as the rewards it could offer, in return for a single-minded focus on career. Gender could still be problematic, however. In her discussion of the predicaments and strategies of women managers, Sheppard (1989, p. 156) considered the precariousness of various gender-management strategies. She argued that whatever strategy ('blending-in' or 'being vigilant') was adopted, women risked having that strategy turned against them. Gender was a highly adaptable and versatile weapon in the gendered competition for promotion in organizations.

It is important to recognize, therefore, the gendered configurations and patterns in the organization that were likely to result from the sorts of responses which the women scientists and engineers were making. The women who avoided management and worked to develop professional specialist careers were actively constructing a career alternative which to an extent was gendered and which would reproduce aspects of occupational segregation in the organization. Such a career could and was being used as a method of combining paid and unpaid-work responsibilities for women. This career choice permitted women to be perceived as less committed to the organization. Similarly, the ideologies of promotion for merit and individualistic achievement would continue to legitimize the gendering of opportunities and positions. The processes of reproduction and gendering within the organization thereby remained disguised and hidden. At the same time, the managerial women were single-minded, competitive, assertive and ambitious. However, because of their promotion success and the ways they had achieved their success, they were continuing to reproduce a particular model of 'successful' management in the organization.

The career actions of individual women and men were working, therefore, to modify *and* to reproduce the gendered processes within the organization. Certainly these women and men were active in constructing career identities, they were not passively adapting to career constraints. The constraints of career were differently conceived and career ambitions were various. However, it is important to remember that identity and structure generate each other. They are mutually reinforcing and reproducing while, at the same time, being mutually capable of affecting and necessitating social change (Evetts, 1992). Changes were apparent: some women were now constructing careers in industrial organizations. Other changes in management and organizational procedures and practices were also a constant feature (see Chapter 9). However, we must continue to ask questions about adaptation and reproduction, particularly in respect of the gendered division of labour within complex organizations. In their actions in respect of career development, for the women and men in the careers history group, aspects of continuity were as apparent as aspects of organizational and social change.

Chapter 8

Gender and Management in Science and Engineering Careers

For women and men in science and engineering, careers are mostly constructed in industrial and other organizations. The exceptions are the relatively small numbers who move into careers in consultancy, as individuals or in partnerships or small firms and often this follows careers in industry. For most scientists and engineers, however, careers are developed by means of promotion progress within organizational career ladders and structures. It is also the case, as has already been noted (see Chapters 5 and 7), that senior positions in organizations require moving from doing the scientific and engineering work to managing others who are doing the work.

For a number of years now, and in a wide range of different occupations and professional contexts, management has been seen to constitute a significant career hurdle for women. While it seems relatively easy for women to gain employment at the lower levels of organizations, it is still proving very difficult for them to reach upper and even middle management (Davidson and Cooper, 1992). In the UK, Hirsh and Jackson (1989) have estimated that out of about three million managers, about one-fifth were women. Definitions of 'manager' are critical here but of the million or so middle and senior managers, only about 4 per cent were women. In 1988, only 5 per cent of the Institute of Directors were women and by 1990, less than 1 per cent of chief executives (Hansard Society Commission, 1990, quoted in Davidson and Cooper, 1992, p. 104).

Other details of women's position in management have also been documented. Wajcman (1994) reported the results of a 1993 study by Gregg and Machin of 533 UK-based companies which found only 8 per cent of top executives were women and their percentage fell dramatically towards the top of the company hierarchy. There is only one woman director of a company with a turnover of more than £600 million, compared with 129 male directors (Institute of Managers and Remuneration Economics, 1993). Women earn significantly less than men for the same jobs. The National Management Salary Survey (Institute of Managers and Remuneration Economics, 1993) demonstrated that women managers and directors continue to be paid less than their male colleagues in every one of six responsibility levels identified. The Institute of Management Survey (1994) recorded a fall (from 10.2 per cent in 1993 to 9.8 per cent in 1994) in the number of women managers. This survey also showed a considerable variation in women's management posts by function, with women managers concentrated in personnel and marketing and least represented in research and development, manufacturing and production (Wajcman, 1994). There are also considerable differences by employment sector with banking, finance and insurance having more women managers. These gender differences are not confined to the UK and similar findings have been recorded in the USA, Europe and Australia (Fagenson, 1993, quoted in Wajcman, 1994).

Theoretical background

A brief history of the theory and practice of women in management since the 1960s has been reviewed by Gray (1994). She has charted the development of the equality movements of the 1960s and 1970s which focused on legislation, policy and practice. The defects of this focus were quickly recognized in that men remained the standard. The position and behaviour of men and the framework of work patterns in organizations remained unchanged and the aim of policies was to bring women 'up to' the men's standard. Women 'found themselves in a world that proclaimed equality of opportunity but defined career paths in the rhythms of a male lifecycle' (Evans, 1989, p. 308, quoted in Gray, 1994, p. 212). This phase resulted in the introduction of a number of 'rational' procedures (e.g. part-time work and flexible working hours) to deal with 'private' issues, as well as practical policies (affirmative action and women-only management training) and theoretical issues (androgyny debates) to deal with policy concerns. The aim, as Gray explained, was to enable 'public' work and career to remain untainted by the emotional, unpredictable and messy nature of private concerns. These initiatives were mainly aimed at women, however, and did nothing to challenge the gendered division of labour in the home and organization, or the barriers to women's move to managerial posts.

The 1980s saw a shift from equality to special treatment for women which emphasized the differences between women and men and recognized the superiority of some women's characteristics for management. This went together with a questioning of simple binary oppositions between women and men and emphasized the need to take contexts and differences in lives and culture into account (Gray, 1994, p. 217). Theories and policies began to focus on the development of management to manage diversity; practical recommendations included employee (as well as customer) surveys and awareness-training to enable people to reach their full potential. Gray has indicated the limitations of this phase as a failure to recognize that valuing differences involves transforming organizations themselves, rather than adapting them or the people in them. The problem was not that women's or men's different approaches to management were not valued, but that difference was defined by power and particularly by power relations in the organization. In this sense, the move into (senior) management positions represented a real 'glass ceiling' for women's careers: 'a barrier so subtle that it is transparent yet so strong that it prevents women and minorities from moving up the management hierarchy' (Morrison and Von Glinow, 1990, p. 200 quoted in Sekaran and Leong 1992, pp. 7–8). In contrast, for men entering predominantly female professions, gender is a positive difference, like stepping on a 'glass escalator' (Williams, 1992).

The 1990s phase in Gray's review is summed up as post-feminist and concerned with the ideologies of individualism and enterprise culture and containing pro-family and heterosexist themes. A rather depressing picture is painted by Gray (1994, p. 224) of women managers still expected to conform to a male model of a successful career and experiencing work overload and an energy deficit (White, Cox and Cooper, 1992). Women still have to manage the tension between work and family and one result is a growing income gap between women:

> a market in which middle-class women buy the labour of working-class women; in which white women buy the labour of black women; and in which enterprise for women means the creation of businesses which essentially service other women in a way which offers no challenge to the sexual division of labour . . . the family and domesticity are added to the list of things we have to manage to be a successful *woman* manager. (Newman, 1991, p. 252, quoted in Gray, 1994, p. 225)

Other researchers have reviewed the different kinds of explanation that have been suggested to account for the gender differences in managerial positions (as suggested by Wajcman, 1994). These explanations are of two main kinds: those that centre on the individual characteristics of women and men themselves; and those that focus on organizational practices and processes. There are, however, many variations within these two main categories and any particular account will usually include aspects of both.

Explanations focusing on individual characteristics

When explanations centre on the individual characteristics of women and men, such explanations can include psychologically based theories of differences in personality traits. Explanations can also focus on differences in the human capital characteristics of the women and men who are building careers, or on differences in amounts of and responsibilities for domestic labour that have to be combined with careers.

When explanations focus on differences in personality traits between women and men, it is argued that women have been socialized into feminine patterns of behaviour which are not suited to the managerial role. In general, women are supposed to lack confidence, drive, ambition and competitiveness when compared with men. This stereotypical and oversimplistic view has been widely discredited, not least because research evidence shows there are very few differences between women and men in cognitive abilities and skills. Blackstone and Weinreich-Haste (1980) found sex differences in cognition had been overstated and had no physiological basis. In fact, the differences within each sex are greater than between the sexes. Herbert and Yost (1979) reviewed the relevant literature and concluded that women do possess the qualities and skills required of management positions (Davidson and Cooper, 1992).

Human capital theory stresses that either women voluntarily choose to invest less or alternatively are not encouraged to acquire the necessary education and training qualifications and career experiences to succeed in promotion applications. They lack both the professional qualifications as well as the breadth and extent of operational experiences in the work organization that have increasingly become necessary for promotion to senior management positions. This explanation can also be challenged. Davidson and Cooper (1983) found that the female manager was generally much better qualified than her male counterpart. Similarly, Crompton and Le Feuvre (1992) have demonstrated how women *can* be bureaucrats and do indeed make use of organizational career structures. Crompton and Sanderson (1990) have shown how women can use the 'qualifications lever' in order to turn the rational bureaucracy of organizational procedures to the benefit of women.

In the rational organization, promotion requirements are often embodied in formal rules and regulations thereby enabling the organization to maintain an image of gender-neutrality. 'The greater the pressure to achieve organizational equality for women, the greater the likelihood, in a situation where sex discrimination is illegal, that the impersonal, formal nature of these rules will be stressed' (Crompton and Sanderson, 1990, p. 115). Where credentials such as job-related skills and educational qualifications are used to define managerial requirements, managerial promotion cannot be denied to those who have them. Crompton and Sanderson argue that if such rational procedures are used by women, a common organizational response is to make such procedures even more rational and systematic. Thus, the acquisition by women of promotion-related criteria makes it very difficult for organizations to deny promotion to aspirant women. Crompton and Sanderson claim that the 'qualifications lever' was being increasingly used by ambitious women and its use has been extended from professions into the internal labour markets of organizations.

Theories based on differences in personality traits and/or human capital investments are both closely related to explanations that focus on differences in the amounts of and responsibilities for domestic labour between women and men. If women are less instrumentally motivated, less interested in career advancement and less committed to paid work generally, this is because they are engaged in considerably higher levels of household labour and caring than men. The explanation, therefore, lies in family structures and the domestic division of labour such that women's lifecycle patterns of work and childbearing and childrearing roles do not fit them for a career in management. This commonsense, rational explanation needs to be extended, however, in order to explain the gendered power relations of women and men in families and why the domestic divisions of labour continue to be unchanged.

It is necessary to acknowledge that ambitions for promotion into managerial positions might be gender-differentiated in so far as the domestic divisions of labour are also widely gender-differentiated. Women with one eye on their family and particularly childcare responsibilities do not consider themselves, nor are they considered to be appropriate candidates in the competition for the limited number of senior managerial promotion positions. In contrast, men with family (and financial) responsibilities are considered entirely appropriate for a salary and responsibility enlargement. This is the belief system which is presented as rational and inevitable but which maintains its force only through the continued separation of private and public work responsibilities and the delegation of caring into the private sphere.

Different attitudes to and perceptions of career and unequal divisions of domestic labour constitute a part of the explanation for the gender differences in the distribution of managerial positions. However, it is necessary to ask why management is considered inappropriate for women – often by women themselves. It is not just the need to work long hours and put the organization's needs first, since organizations could adapt to and devise ways of coping with women's family responsibilities if they needed to. Perhaps we should ask why is management continually portrayed in particular ways, such that women, as well as men, are required to adapt and conform to the image of the dedicated manager? The power of the cultural stereotype of management has been assessed by Powell (1988) who concluded that androgyny (same combination of masculine and feminine characteristics) was probably the best model. Yet stereotypical beliefs about men, women and management continue to influence promotion decisions as well as the number of women who put themselves forward for promotion. It might be that gender-different attitudes to and aspirations for managerial promotion in the career are themselves a product of gendered processes within the organization itself.

Explanations focusing on organizational processes

The second category of explanations are those that focus on the practices and processes within organizations. Within work organizations, competition for promotion into managerial positions can be restricted to those already working in the organization. In this way an internal labour market (see Chapter 1) develops which constitutes a career structure whereby some professional workers progress and achieve promotion in their careers whereas others continue to develop practitioner careers. Crompton and Sanderson (1990) have examined the operation of different professional internal labour markets and have argued that historically women have been excluded from access to such career structures. In the past this was done through occupational segregation. Where men and women were in gender-segregated jobs, it was easy to deny women access to managerial promotion positions. However, when professional women are denied promotion in jobs which supposedly recruit on the basis of gender-neutral attributes, other mechanisms and processes are required to support and reproduce the unequal gender outcomes.

These processes have been conceptualized in several different ways. Witz (1988, 1990) has described the processes as ones of social closure. Using Parkin's definition of modes of closure (1974), exclusion is described as a means of mobilizing power for the purpose of claiming promotional resources and opportunities. 'Gendered strategies of exclusionary closure serve to create women as a class of ineligibles and secure for men privileged access to rewards and opportunities' (Witz, 1988, p. 76).

Atkinson and Delamont (1990), using data on professional scientists, have argued that core sets of (male) professionals are responsible for legitimating and disseminating information about professional competence and expertise. Such core-set members are also responsible for selecting candidates for promotion. The problem for women is not their human capital, namely women's investment in technical knowledge and expertise. Rather the problem is professional contact, style and legitimacy: what Atkinson (1983) called 'indeterminate' knowledge and what Bourdieu (1986) called the 'habitus' of professional and organizational occupations. In this sense, women's failure to secure managerial positions is due '*not* to their lack of technical skills necessary for the jobs, but to their perceived failure to behave in ways which reveal their mastery of the indeterminate: that is their failure to share the habitus' (Atkinson and Delamont, 1990, p. 107).

Professional women have been acquiring the skills and the credentials necessary for promotion to senior positions. However, within organizations, access to managerial positions does not depend on formal credentials alone. Collins (1979) has examined the 'property in positions'; he has argued that 'the one who makes it to the top is the organizational politician, concerned above all with informal ties, manoeuvring toward the crucial gatekeepers, avoiding the organizational contingencies that trap the less wary' (Collins, 1979, p. 31).

All these processes depend on the supposed gender-neutrality of promotion structures (Crompton and Sanderson, 1990). The authority of the organization (rational-legal authority, Weber, 1948) is legitimated by rules that include open competition and the possession of appropriate qualifications, skills and experience by candidates for promotion posts. Thus the low representation of women in managerial positions is explained in terms of gender-neutral rules such as those relating to formal qualifications, length of service, work experience, commitment to the organization and aspirations for career. The rationality of such procedures is indisputable and therein lies the ideological power of the organization.

In addition to explanations that focus on the processes and practices of organizations there is a further body of literature which emphasizes the cultural forms that are submerged in organizational decisions. Wajcman (1994) has explained how it is through a set of cultural representations and meanings that people construct their understandings of the gendered structure of work and opportunity within organizations. Thus gender is mapped on to organizational authority such that women are better suited to personnel than to other management functions. Similarly, the necessary scripts are provided for gender-appropriate behaviours and attitudes. Managerial work is thereby presented as decisive, aggressive and competitive, needing a tough, forceful leader. The image is intrinsically male and produces a close identification between men and management. In this way, women are marginalized and out of place; management is a 'foreign territory' for them (Marshall, 1984).

The careers history respondents

The experiences of the respondents in the careers history group illustrated many of the themes and issues which have been described in respect of gender and management in the research literature. Some of their experiences were shared with women and men in other professions and types of employment. Other experiences were particularly associated with management in complex and hierarchical work organizations. This section will consider four related aspects. First, the respondents had absorbed the rationality and logic of the organization and this will be described. Second, the respondents' perceptions of differences in styles of management will be assessed. Third, some of the cultural dilemmas of management in organizations will be examined. Fourth, the women in senior management positions will be considered and their different responses to the cultural dilemmas of management will be described.

The rationality of the organization

The previous section has considered how organizational processes depend on the supposed gender-neutrality of promotion and selection by merit for managerial positions. The authority of the organization is legitimated by rules which include open competition and the promotion of candidates who possess appropriate qualifications, skills and experience. Any written-down criteria of merit are also accompanied and enforced by a set of commonsense taken-for-granted assumptions, values and ideas. By these means, the low representation of women in managerial positions is explained in terms of gender-neutral rules such as those relating to formal qualifications, breadth and extent of work experience, a reluctance to put themselves forward for promotion, personal skills and managerial attributes, and commitment to the organization. Women and men absorb such explanations and use them to account for their own promotion positions and experiences.

The men in the careers history group were persuaded by such logic. They were mostly sympathetic and prepared to be understanding about the dual responsibilities of their women colleagues. This meant, however, that women's promotion ambitions would have to be 'appropriate' in order to compensate. Women should be realistic in terms of what they could and could not do. In general, managerial positions, except at the lower team or section leader levels, were perceived as inappropriate for women with dual allegiances. Commonsense required management posts to be occupied by those with a more than full-time commitment to the organization.

It was interesting to observe that the women respondents had also absorbed the same rationality and logic in explaining their own and others' career positions in respect of management in the organization. This was the same for the women with children as well as for those who were childfree.

> Promotion will become more difficult now to go further. I think that the barriers are going to be *now* because I think they start looking at you as going to have a family and not be committed or maybe her commitment's somewhere else. That isn't how they look at anybody else, but I think they'll start to think about it more for me. (Lindsay, no children)

> Women can return to their work (after having children) but I think your career development at that time is really severely hampered. You're seen as unreliable because you have a dual role. You might have to go off to take your children to the dentist or do all those other things. That does not put your job first. So you are compromising your job for other things, so you are not at the beck and call of work. I think that is seen as a problem. (Susan, no children)

> At the moment I am reasonably happy because with a small child I need to concentrate on the home a little more so I need a job where I feel I am experienced and I don't really need to put 120 per cent effort in. But in two or three years time when she is going off to school, then that is maybe when I am thinking well I want a little more, a change of direction or I need to widen my horizons a little bit more. (Sarah, one child)

These women, like their male colleagues, had come to terms with the conception of management as unidimensional and of professional managers as being without family obligations and responsibilities, at least while they were at work. They had accepted that women with family ties and partnership expectations were probably unsuited to undertake the responsibilities of management in the organization.

Management styles

When researchers have focused on management and on gender differences in management, the question of leadership style frequently becomes the point at issue. Gender differences in leadership style were examined in a preliminary way in Chapter 1 where it was argued that, although there are obvious differences between managers in the ways in which leadership is operationalized, few of the differences are obviously gender-related. Differences in style are easily demonstrated as managers head their departments, sections and teams in different ways. According to Ball (1987, p. 82) some managers rely on their own personal influence, conviction and leadership qualities; others emphasize bureaucratic procedures, delegating authority, managing through committee structures and establishing clear lines of hierarchical delegation and responsibility; others rely more on the power of their position, managing through control and rules and motivating through sanctions, rewards and punishments. Most managers use a combination of styles, managing different people in different ways and adjusting styles to circumstances. Most managers are of necessity middle-people who act as go-betweens. They are required to carry out corporate plans and decisions from above and operationalize them in their departments and teams. Similarly, they are usually required to convey the concerns and anxieties of those teams to the company directors who are the policy and decision-makers. The organizational task of the manager has been perceived by Ball as the need to achieve and maintain control (domination) while encouraging and ensuring social order and commitment (integration).

The difficulties of demonstrating clear, consistent gender differences in leadership styles have been acknowledged in the research literature. Shakeshaft (1979, 1985) used a Leadership Behaviour Description Questionnaire and found no difference between women and men on 12 dimensions of leadership behaviour (representation, demand conciliation, tolerance of uncertainty, persuasiveness, initiation of structure, toleration of freedom, role assumption, consideration, production emphasis, predictive accuracy, integration and superior orientation). She went on to argue, however, that there might be substantial contrasts and contradictory findings between studies which used specially devised questionnaires (like her own) and studies which used observation, work diaries and more qualitative and smaller-scale research techniques. In a similar way, Ball (1987) analysed four ideal types of leadership style (interpersonal, managerial, political-adversarial and political-authoritarian). In his subsequent elaboration and illustration of these styles, he does not refer to gender differences. It is necessary to conclude from this that gender was an insignificant variable in differentiating these types.

There are then no easily demonstrated gender differences in management and leadership styles. It is obviously the case that women and men do the same things when they manage. The women would not have been selected for management unless they could complete the tasks and comprehend and master the managerial culture. Gender differences in terms of the definitions of objectives, perceptions of the organization and task completion, are not significant.

The scientists and engineers in the careers history study responded in different ways to a question about differences in management styles. The engineers were more inclined than the scientists to attribute any differences to personality rather than to gender.

> Other than imprinting your own personal view on the job, I can't think there are any differences. (Kate, engineering manager)

> I probably do things differently, yes, but I haven't ever sat back and thought well how would I deal with this if I were a man, no. (Frances, engineering director)

The men were also more concerned to attribute differences to personality rather than to gender. The large majority of women respondents were, however, convinced that there were significant gender differences. Examples were readily given from the women's own experiences both of management itself and of being managed. The main differences were perceived to be of four main kinds: women were less confrontational; more considerate; less formal; and better able to manage numerous things at once. These characteristics were perceived to be a great advantage in the processes of management in the organization.

> I think I am more conciliatory than a man would be. But I have noticed a lot of change [in me] since I have had this new job. Before then I felt I could be more thoughtful and considerate and more worried about people's feelings. Since then I have had to be a lot more assertive and I have felt myself being more managing. I think I have changed the way the departments are run. I have changed the relationships we have with other departments. I have tried to be much more proactive. I had to battle to get a proper system of documentation . . . I am very well aware that I am harder than I was a year ago. (Penny, department manager)

> I use the fact that I am female and that they are not going to get verbally abusive towards me, and to make the whole thing friendly. If a man is overly friendly the other male managers seem to think he is

a walkover, but if a woman approaches it in a friendly manner they are far more happy to accept it. In general they seem far happier to accept my criticisms than if a man criticizes them. In our summing-up session they calm down far easier if I make a comment to them than if any of the men in the group make a comment. I deliberately use that. (Lilian, section manager)

I think, actually I know, that I pay more attention to the people within the job rather than the job itself. I try to strike the balance between being people-orientated and task-orientated. . . . I think it actually achieves better results. A lot of the groups I have managed I have not known a lot about what they actually do, but I've managed to get a lot out of the people. I think a lot of that is just because of directing effort towards them. I suppose you are making them feel valuable, making them feel their jobs are worthwhile and the company attributes value to them. (Vivian, engineering manager)

This is something which has been discussed by my staff. I am much more reasonable if they want to take time off. For example, one of my staff his brother had cancer and just my attitude, the fact that I would allow him to ring him up at home, that he could talk to me about the problem and was quite happy to cry in front of me. I am quite understanding if the woman who works for me needs time off, she can ring me at home. I think they feel with the men that is not possible. So I think I have a better working relationship with my staff. (Susan, principal scientist)

One comment that has been made to me and I would agree, that I care to my own detriment about people. I haven't got the killer-instinct of some men. About three years ago, and things *have* now changed, I thought I did not want to become a manager because people did not seem to matter. I think I would accept a management role now because there is more caring in management. But I don't think that's female; I think that's me. (Mary, principal technologist)

I do think there is a difference with the way you do the job. If I were to call a meeting of my staff, I am much less likely to use a structured agenda. We get through the business in the same time but we tend to follow it through rather than having a written out agenda . . . But women are different from men in that sort of sense because they tend to ramble all over the place and they still get the job done in the end. (Marie, department head)

Individuals are always different but having looked at the way men work, men are very good at pursuing single tasks, very single-mindedly, and women are much better at juggling a lot of little tasks and getting them done altogether, but maybe not as single-minded as men are. I do think women are far better organisers than men [laughter]. (Ann, principal technologist)

In general, then, the women scientists were the most emphatic about the importance of gender differences in management styles. Most of the women engineers were also in agreement although some of the women engineers, like all the men engineers and scientists, were inclined to attribute differences to personality rather than to gender. The differences most often illustrated were those which perceived women managers to be more conciliatory and less confrontational; more considerate, caring, sympathetic and approachable; more informal, flexible and sensitive; and better able to manage numerous tasks. All these characteristics were perceived to be a great asset for management in the organization.

What is significant about these perceptions is an emphasis on style rather than on gender differences as such. The objective in clarifying different perceptions is not to enable a claim that either women or men make better managers. Where differences are explored, however, we get a clearer understanding of what are the important aspects of management, particularly for those who are managed. We are then in a better position to ask which is the best style of management and leadership in that department/section at that time. One criterion of good management is that it should relate both to the organization's and the participants' needs. Such needs are both structural (continuity and replacement) and cultural (including working relations and practices). The management needs will vary according to external (economic) conditions, corporate climate and policy, as well as with the internal dynamics of particular groups of people and their working relationships. Circumstances will alter and managerial needs will change within the organization.

The cultural dilemmas for women managers

The central question here is the culture of work in organizations and how this shapes gender relations at work. In its day-to-day operation the organization is made up of a set of procedures and processes which are essentially male-defined. Men's influence is embedded in rules and regulations, in formal job specifications and descriptions and in functional roles and interactions. Promotion-successful women have to absorb and operationalize these rules in order to take on managerial responsibilities. The gendered structure of work and opportunity within organizations also provides the scripts for gender-appropriate behaviours and attitudes (Wajcman, 1994). These scripts detail the way people talk to each other, how they interact formally and informally and their taken-for-granted assumptions, values and ideas. These determine our understandings of what is and is not appropriate work for women and for men and our commonsense appreciations of what are 'natural' behaviours and aspirations.

One of the most fascinating aspects of the culture of management in the organization is that it is impossible for women to meet the conflicting and contradictory expectations confronting them. Thus, in respect of childcare, whatever the woman does, she cannot meet the expectations of others and herself in respect of 'appropriate' behaviour. The mothers in the careers history study were well aware of the contradictions.

> I think it can be quite difficult for women because I think people are very judgemental over what you do about children. You can't win because if you don't have them that is not right. If you have them and leave them at home that's not right. I don't feel that anyone can win in that situation. I believe I probably am the nearest one to hitting it right. I feel the men don't really know how to judge me for that. I think they are quite hard on women who go back to work with young children, well young babies. (Penny, department manager, two children)

What is equally important is that in respect of management in the organization, and particularly senior management, the expectations for women are totally contradictory and overwhelmingly problematic. Thus senior managers have to be tough, strong, forceful leaders. Men can appropriately display and exhibit such qualities but for women such behaviour is 'unnatural'.

> You have to be extremely tough and usually a total bitch to be able to get through. You have got to be prepared to stand on other people, to be the sort of person I couldn't live with myself if I was. The women who are successful are mostly people who you wouldn't want to know, because they have had such a tough fight. If you want to move into a senior management position in a big company you are going to have to be very tough. (Sarah-Jane, technical information officer)

The dilemma, however, is that toughness in women is inappropriate gender behaviour. It is not only work colleagues (female and male) who disapprove. The organization develops its own systems and procedures for sanctioning gender-inappropriate behaviour.

> Talking to the Personnel Manager a little while ago, he said that the problem with most women who are wanting to look after a small work force is they become almost aggressive – they try and make out that they are as hard as the men are, and that they are able to control staff as easy as men can, and that they won't get emotionally upset if they have to discipline someone. And he says they go over the top,

that they become so hard that they are unapproachable, and that is one of the reasons they get marked down. And that is one of the reasons why there are so few women managers around. (Lilian, documentation manager)

There are, then, significant cultural dilemmas for women managers in the organization. Women can appropriately display the qualities of conciliation, caring and informality discussed as advantages in the previous section. The difficulty is that these very qualities will be perceived as disadvantages in the competition for senior management positions. Yet those women who *do* display toughness and aggression will in turn be perceived as too hard and unapproachable and as women they will be marked down for such qualities. One of the organizations in the careers history study was using psychometric tests in order to select individuals for managerial posts. It could be interesting to study how any gender differences in scores would be perceived. Probably only the women managers would have to walk the tightrope between being feminine enough on the one hand and tough enough on the other, in order to succeed in management posts.

The senior women managers

A recent survey of senior managers in Britain (Institute of Management, 1992) illustrated how women who break through the 'glass ceiling' do so at considerable personal cost. One-third of the women managers in the survey were unmarried (8 per cent of the men); 12 per cent were divorced or separated (5 per cent of the men); nearly half of the women had never had a caring responsibility (12 per cent of the men). Management and particularly senior management seems to present women with formidable career and personal requirements.

In the careers history study, two of the women were identified as being in senior management (or higher) positions, one at Airmax and one at Marlands. Frances, already a director at Airmax, denied any difficulties. She was not aware of any problems in being able to reconcile her position as a senior manager and a woman in professional engineering. In this respect Frances' career identity matched that of the most senior woman manager interviewed by Sheppard. Sheppard's most successful respondent said gender was never a factor because she ignored it (Sheppard, 1989; p. 144). Similarly, Frances' career had involved a single-minded focus on promotion and achievement in her career.

J.E: Has being a woman affected your career?
Frances: I have never really been aware of it and I'm not sure whether that means that I'm just thick-skinned or whether it's because I have always been the only one so far that it becomes a way of

life. I really do forget about it and it's been rather nice when people, colleagues, have perhaps commented that quite often they forget. One boss, I had, made a comment. I don't think it was meant to be complimentary but I remember it with fondness. He said I think you are a man in a woman's body [laughter]. No it hasn't not really. I honestly think there are as many pros as there are cons. I think for men and women the pros and cons are quite different, but I think they net out to zero, I really do.

Frances' career had involved a single-minded dedication to promotion in the organization. She had a long-standing partnership and was childfree by choice. She had responsibilities for an elderly mother but was not directly involved in caring. The personal aspects of her identity were fitted around her professional work responsibilities. She was dedicated to the company and to her career.

Sylvia, at Marlands, had also concentrated on achieving promotion in the organization, though her dedication was not single-minded and her personal circumstances were different to Frances'. Sylvia was very supportive of her husband's extremely successful career and she was childfree but not through choice. Sylvia did report difficulties in management experiences of the kind this chapter has explored.

I tried for about six years to get a job in production until I was told on the basis of psychometric testing that I was not suitable as a production manager because I wasn't aggressive enough. They have this idea that you have to be something like Attila the Hun to be a good production manager, which if you actually talk to the operators they don't like . . . Promotion has to be very much self-initiated within the company for any sort of progression. If you don't apply for vast quantities of jobs they don't think you are interested.

The experiences of these two women illustrate the different ways in which senior management positions had been achieved in the two organizations in this study. One way was through single-minded career dedication so that personal relationships were fitted around and perceived as being supportive of managerial commitments and responsibilities. This still required a deliberate act of self-presentation and of balancing; of being assertive enough to demonstrate senior management potential though not being too aggressive. Another way was through less single-minded dedication to promotion and attempting instead to balance public and private aspects of identity. This strategy also involved daily attempts at balance, this time in gender and senior management expectations and requirements.

Thus, of the two women senior managers in the careers history study, both were walking the cultural tightrope which management in the organization presented for women. One (Frances) had prioritized the public over personal aspects of her identity and was balancing aspects of self-presentation. She denied that gender was a problem. The other (Sylvia) was balancing aspects of her public and personal life and was attempting daily to negotiate such a balance. She perceived gender to have been problematic in her own career.

The increased use of psychometric testing in organizations presents an additional gender-relevant requirement. This could be perceived as another 'qualifications lever' (Crompton and Sanderson, 1990) which women will have to learn to use to their own advantage as they have learned to use other rational merit-based promotion criteria such as additional qualifications and experience. The subjective interpretations that might be made of gender comparability in results, in such tests, is in need of further clarification, however.

Conclusion

This chapter has examined some of the gender differences and the difficulties, particularly for women, posed by management in science and engineering careers. In general, management was characterized as particularly problematic for women. Both women and men are reluctant to be managed by a woman. The difficulties increase with senior management positions; both organizational structures and the culture of senior management constitute formidable obstacles for women.

The experiences of the women and men in the careers history group demonstrated some of the difficulties. The women perceived themselves to have particular styles of leadership which were advantageous to the organization. These very qualities could, however, be seen as disadvantageous for those seeking senior management positions. Yet, at the same time, toughness and assertion in women fitted uneasily with expectations of appropriate gender behaviour. Such contradictory expectations were clearly impossible for most women to reconcile.

Senior management probably constitutes the real 'glass ceiling' for women's careers in organizations. The difficulties which career promotion into management poses for women have been recognized ('Opportunity 2000', for example) and certain proposals for change have been made to improve women's career opportunities. Recommendations include the setting of targets for the recruitment and promotion of women into senior management positions; the expansion and development of anti-discriminatory practices, procedures, regulations and legislation; an emphasis and recognition of the positive attributes women bring to management; and the encouragement of more sharing between partners in the unpaid-work tasks of domestic labour and caring responsibilities.

Some changes have resulted. There is now a heightened awareness that gender inequality in managerial promotions is a problem, not just for women themselves but for the organizations that employ them. However, recommendations like those listed cannot resolve the cultural contradictions which management poses for women. Taking the above recommendations as examples, the problems are easily indicated. It is clear that targets cannot be achieved unless the prior issues that make women reluctant managers are addressed. Legislation and anti-discriminatory procedures can improve awareness but can also increase the practices of avoidance and evasion on the part of promotion panels (see Cockburn, 1991). An emphasis on gender differences in style and managerial effectiveness can only lead to an exaggeration of gender-stereotyping which is ultimately unhelpful. A change in the distribution of domestic and personal responsibilities would obviously be of practical assistance to many women, but changes in the private sphere of home and family are the most difficult to achieve. And even if such changes were effected, this would do nothing to address the conception of management as unidimensional and the relegation of caring tasks into the separate private arena. More sharing in the home might even increase the numbers of men who would become reluctant managers (Scase and Goffee, 1989)!

It is certainly the case that organizations are increasingly developing criterion-referenced schemes for the allocation of merit money and even lower-level promotion positions. It has been assumed that such 'objective' schemes will make promotion procedures more open and more equally available to both women and men in organizations. This does not necessarily mean that such rational procedures can be applied in achieving access to managerial promotions, however. In the companies the careers history respondents worked for, promotion on the technologist or scientist scales *was* criterion-referenced and the characteristics required were formalized in writing and copies were distributed to each graduate employee. Promotion into management positions was different, however. In the case of management, individuals were approached and were 'invited to apply'. Through the maintenance of management posts outside the rational criterion-referenced procedures of early promotion scales, the selection characteristics for management were able to continue to be subjective, ill-defined and mysterious. Management posts could not be achieved by aspirant women and men through the rational application of the qualifications lever.

The use of psychometric-testing procedures for the selection of individuals with appropriate management potential might similarly be perceived as questionable. Clearly this is an attempt to 'objectify' selection processes in order to legitimate the rationality of organizational procedures. It has, however, been demonstrated how the same qualities of toughness, assertion and aggression can be differently perceived in women and men candidates for promotion posts. Such a qualifications lever has to be operationalized differently by women and men.

There is also another difficultly with the qualifications lever. The intention of using the rational procedures of defined criteria such as additional qualifications, wide experience, leadership qualities and mobility requires women to adapt to already existing conceptions and stereotypes of dedicated management. Women must match up to such criteria and achieve the additional experiences and qualifications – and have the requisite personalities – in order to achieve promotion into management. Some women are prepared to do this and have succeeded in management posts. The personal costs for some of these women are high, however, and other professional women and men are not prepared to steer and adjust their careers towards such a unidimensional conception of management. These other women and men wish rather to continue to develop different aspects of themselves and instead to build multidimensional careers.

There are also other difficulties. Organizations themselves are constantly changing as they have to adapt and adjust their procedures in an increasingly competitive and international market. As a consequence, management itself is being changed within the organization. Chapter 9 considers these aspects of change and explores the gender and career consequences for women and men scientists and engineers.

Chapter 9

Gender and Career in Science and Engineering

This book has explored and illustrated some of the ideas and concepts which have been perceived as central in the examination of careers in science and engineering in large industrial organizations. It has also focused on some of the major gender differences in such careers. The career *experiences* of 41 women and men scientists, programmers and engineers, working for two industrial organizations, have been used to explore explanatory processes, not to produce statistical generalizations. The final chapter has two objectives. The first is to return to the themes of culture/structure/action dimensions of careers examined in Chapter 1 and to use these to summarize and comment on the main aspects of stability and change in the gender experiences of careers. The second objective, using some of the theoretical concepts developed in Chapter 2, is to examine how the organizations themselves might be changing the structural contexts for careers in science and engineering. This will involve an exploration of how gender, career, management, class, profession and organization have interacted and are interacting to produce new as well as old career patterns and forms of occupational segregation.

Stability and change in gender experiences of career

It is necessary to begin by re-emphasizing the mutually reinforcing nature of the three dimensions of career: structure, culture and action. We need to have constantly in mind the interrelations of these aspects of career, of how structure and culture arise out of actions and how actions are influenced by structure and culture (Bourdieu and Wacquant, 1992). What people do in their careers always presupposes some kind of pre-existing structure (promotion ladders, rules of behaviour, cultural expectations, etc.) but, in what they do, people simultaneously recreate the structure and culture anew or alternatively new structures emerge and are developed. The processes of structuration (Giddens, 1984) and the possibilities of reproduction or change through the creation of new structures need to be considered.

For the most part it is through external and internally generated change that modifications in career actions and expectations can bring about changes in organizational career structures and cultures. Alternatively, changes in organizational career structures can necessitate alterations in career actions and expectations. Career experiences and career structures and cultures have an internal dynamic and a mutual interdependence. Change has to be included in our explanations, as it has to be incorporated in new reality-defining structures and systems in the separate organizations and professional workplaces and in the experiences of individual women and men. In the analysis of change, the experiences of actors are fundamental. When sufficient numbers of practitioners/employees alter 'established' career patterns via their actions, career structures and systems are thereby modified and changed (Gunz, 1989). Experiences of career are part of the same mutually reinforcing process whereby actions and structures both interact and reinforce a career outcome. Conditions of change form the best contexts in which to observe the interrelation of structural, cultural and action dimensions of career.

Change is on-going and continuous. Elements of gender differences and disadvantages (like wage differentials and unequal promotion prospects) continue to be reproduced, but not in precisely the same structural or cultural forms or contexts. Experiences of career (for both women and men) are changing fundamentally. When career experiences and expectations change, then changes in career structures are likely to follow since career action and behaviour is the generator of career structures and systems. Change in the cultural influences on careers might be slower to affect and sustain. The controlling force of cultural imperatives constitutes a check and a brake on both action and structural impetuses for change. Cultural assumptions, stereotypes and moral prescriptions will eventually change, however, and ideologies will adapt to sustain new structural career patterns.

It is necessary to emphasize that change represents opportunities as well as constraints for career builders. Explanations in terms of culture and structure have tended to emphasize the career constraints, the career determinants, particularly for women. The constraints are real and should not be minimized. Cultural and structural processes do constrain the career opportunities for women, more so than for men. But the career actions of women as well as men *can* lead to the creation of new career structures, as well as the reproduction of existing ones (Knorr-Cetina and Cicourel, Eds, 1981). When sufficient numbers of practitioner/employees alter 'established' career patterns via their actions, usually spurred by structural, organizational and professional change, career structures and promotion systems are altered and modified, ultimately resulting in cultural change.

Career actions can alter structures just as structures affect actions. We must not underestimate the resistances of women and men actors themselves in the organizations and professions in which they are building careers. The analysis of cultural and structural constraints to women's careers must be supplemented by a recognition of the variety and variation of women's responses. This results in untidy contradictions in work places and organizations which represent actors' attempts to challenge the constraints to women's, as well as to men's, careers.

Previous chapters have highlighted at least three substantive issues which are of direct relevance to the careers of women and men scientists and engineers in industrial organizations. In respect of these three issues, aspects of both stability and change are apparent and are important influences in gender differences in the experience of career. The three issues are listed and then examined in turn:

1 public and private aspects of careers;
2 managerial aspects of careers;
3 the culture of career and promotion.

Public and private aspects of careers

The conflict and stress that occur when trying to balance work and family roles has been well documented in Britain and particularly in the USA (Barker and Allen, Eds, 1976; Finch and Groves, Eds, 1983; Sharpe, 1984; Adams and Winston, 1980; Scanzoni, 1978; Goldsmith, Ed., 1989; Ferber, O'Farrell and La Rue, Eds, 1991). In earlier studies this was assumed to be a problem for women (Myrdal and Klein, 1968) because of the cultural association between caring and feminine identity. Later studies have confirmed that, although women's careers have been most affected, the way forward is to regard work-family issues as universal, not just as women's concern.

As women form an increasing part of the labour market, they show greater attachment to it in terms of the proportion of their lives spent in paid employment. Young women as school-leavers are becoming better qualified for paid work and are entering a wider range of occupations on more equal terms. Slower and more resistant to change are the private worlds of partnerships and families. But here, too, men as well as women are requiring change. Working fathers and mothers are torn between the conflicting demands of their jobs and the desire to see more of their families. Some men as well as many women would give up salary and promotion to have more family and personal time. But both men and women are affected by work-family concerns on a daily basis and avoid jobs that involve relocation (Scase and Goffee, 1989; Thompson, Thomas and Maier, 1992).

Some work organizations have reported increases in the numbers of managers, both male and female, who refuse to relocate even for promotions. A study at Mobil Oil Corporation (reported in Thompson, Thomas and Maier, 1992) found that Mobil men were more likely than Mobil women to refuse requests for relocation. This is partly explained by the fact that 80 per cent of the male managers in the study had dependent children while this applied to only 10 per cent of the female managers. It is clear that the men and women of the corporation (Kanter, 1977) were differently experiencing work-family conflicts and developing different strategies for resolving them. Mobil men were experiencing high levels of conflict which for some led to a refusal to relocate while the Mobil women were anticipating such conflict and resolving it by postponing or avoiding parenthood (Thompson, Thomas and Maier, 1992, p. 62). In a similar way, Scase and Goffee's 'reluctant managers' (1989) were mostly male since there were fewer women, more of whom were single and/or childfree. It is important to emphasize, therefore, that women who are successful so far in promotion and career terms are perhaps a particular group of women: namely, women who have rejected or limited the demands that private, family lives make on careers. As a career pattern, this presents women and men with an impossible choice and is probably unsustainable. If, in order to succeed in career terms, both women and men must severely curtail the demands of personal and family lives, then future prospects are bleak. We must do much better than this if we are to make best use of human capital, both male and female, in the contexts of work and family.

These issues are not easy to resolve and solutions have not been forthcoming. Legislation and social-policy directives have demonstrated how limited are political and legislative directives in producing attitudinal and social change. In the very different ideological climate of the USA, where individuals and organizations are left to cope with conflict and stress without State or federal regulation, the case for change has been justified in economic terms as the best way of 'enhancing the productivity and profitability of organizations' (Sekaran and Leong, 1992, p. xi). What is needed, therefore, for both women's and men's careers is some new way of reconciling the experiences of the unpaid- and paid-work aspects of careers to the benefit of both women and men. Women have so far been under-represented in the promotion positions of paid work but they have almost monopolized the caring experiences of parenthood. Men have been over-represented in the senior management positions of careers but have denied themselves or been denied the pleasures as well as the responsibilities of full partnership and parenthood.

There are some signs of change. Men are now recognizing and having to reconcile work and family demands. When it comes to the division of labour in the home, however, despite some optimistic forecasting (Young and Willmott, 1973), most research suggests that women still do the large majority of tasks associated with housework and childcare (Edgell, 1980; Moss and Fonda, Eds, 1980; Sharpe, 1984; Yeandle, 1984). Thus while men are increasingly making career decisions with their partners and families in mind, nevertheless most of them do not do their share of household and childcare tasks. This makes it more difficult for most women to be serious contenders in the competition for career promotion.

There have also been some signs of change in the way work organizations operate. In the competitive market place, organizations cannot change unilaterally and all changes have to be justified in terms of economic efficiency rather than social justice. Thompson, Thomas and Maier (1992, p. 63) have described some of these organizational initiatives in the USA which they list as programmes for (i) dependent care; (ii) parental leave; (iii) spouse relocation; and (iv) alternative work schedules such as flexitime, job-sharing and part-time work. In Britain some of the problems associated with initiatives such as these have been examined by Cockburn (1991). Such schemes are severely limited, however, if only or predominantly women participate. Where such initiatives assume or imply that the man is the main career-builder, the difficulties for women's careers continue.

It is necessary, therefore, to alter the imagery and culture associated with the 'successful' career. The careers of successful women and men have tended to be unidimensional. Those on the fast track in organizations and the professions have been required to concentrate exclusively on the job. They have been required to act as if they had no other loyalties and certainly no family life (Kanter, 1977). The de-gendering of career requires a more positive attitude to the multifaceted career where the management of different identities can be recognized and rewarded with career progress and development. In order to achieve this shift, however, we must also consider the second issue: namely, the unidimensional conception of management in the organization.

Managerial aspects of careers

In one sense, experiences of career are experiences of promotion: that is, of movements upwards through hierarchically organized job positions. In this sense, experiences of career are experiences of movements into management, of changes in work from doing the job to the managing and administration of others who are doing the job. This was particularly the case for the organizational scientists and engineers in this study. This conception has always applied in organizational careers where hierarchies of posts and positions have constituted promotion structures and individuals have developed linear careers through such structures. Increasingly this conception is also relevant to other professional careers. Many professionals have in any case always worked in large-scale organizations and for those professionals working in smaller group practices, issues of advancement and progress are increasingly influencing career choices and decisions. Management has come to represent career progress for large numbers of professional workers.

However, there are considerable gender differences in the distribution of management, hence promotion, positions. The proportion of women who hold management, executive or administrative positions has been rising consistently since the 1970s. These women tend to hold lower level posts, however, and are concentrated in positions with less authority and responsibility than men (see next section). One explanation lies in the nature of management itself. Powell (1988) described how the job of manager has been defined as masculine, with men seeing themselves and being seen by promotion panels as more suited for it than women. Powell examined the influence of gender stereotyping which suggests that men are more appropriate for hierarchical leadership roles than women and find the intense competition for such positions more conducive. Other researchers have sought the explanation more in the nature of organizations themselves (Hearn *et al.*, Eds, 1989) and in the general patriarchal system which diverts and resists attempts to introduce change in organizations (Marshall, 1984; Cockburn, 1991).

Gender differences in management styles have been a preoccupation of researchers (see Chapter 8). Following a review of research into managerial behaviour, Powell (1988, p. 165) concluded that the sex differences that have been found were few and tended to cancel each other out. For Powell the only significant difference between managerial men and women was the environment in which they operated with sex imbalances contributing to stereotypical preconceptions and cultural dilemmas for managerial women. However, at the British Psychological Society Conference in January 1992, contributors were still arguing that there were fundamental differences in the qualities which men and women brought to management (Clement, 1992a, 1992b). As a result, it is claimed that women experienced a contradiction between their formal managerial authority and their feminine identities which militated against the practice of that authority.

It is certainly the case that *beliefs* about gender differences have a great impact on careers in organizations. Promotion in the career depends on organizational representatives, managers, assessors and appraisers evaluating the suitability of candidates for merit awards and promotion. Managers evaluate the performance of their subordinates. Promotion decisions are based on evaluations of past performance, future potential and comparisons between candidates for promotion. Promotion is inevitably competitive since in hierarchical pyramidal career structures there are only a modest number of middle-ranking managerial positions and very few at the top. In such a structure, others' evaluations materially affect the progress of an individual in an organization. Evaluations are based on beliefs about what an individual is like and gender continues to influence such evaluations. Stereotypical beliefs that women are either more expressive or alternatively too aggressive, while men are more task-orientated and better natural leaders, have a marked impact on promotion decisions about managerial posts. Beliefs about gender differences, however lacking in research evidence, have a continuing effect on promotion prospects for careers.

Proposals and recommendations for equalizing career opportunities in management have been forthcoming, largely determined by where the explanation for gender imbalance is seen to lie. Thus, those who see the problem as being discrimination in organizations have proposed stronger equal opportunities legislation, the setting of recruitment and promotion targets and the notion of a 'qualifications lever' (Crompton and Sanderson, 1990) whereby the qualifications and qualities required for promotion posts are specified thereby enabling women, as well as men, to seek to acquire them. Those who explain the gender imbalance in management by reference to gender stereotypes have suggested androgynous management as the ideal, which 'blends behaviours previously deemed to belong exclusively to men or women' (Sargent, 1981, p. 2). Powell has argued (1988, p. 170) that 'If an androgynous manager is defined as one who has the capability to be either high or low in both task-orientated and people-orientated behaviour, most management theorists would agree that better managers are androgynous.' It is also argued that androgynous managers are actually higher in behaviourial flexibility and adaptability and thereby better fitted to organizational needs which increasingly require managers who are adaptable and multifunctional. The new manager will therefore have to decide to be more task-orientated or people-orientated depending on an evaluation of subordinates' needs and situational factors such as the firm's general economic circumstances and the organization's climate.

In general, then, it seems that we need to change and to broaden and extend our conceptions of 'good' management. For individuals, both men and women, there is more to life than a career. Obsession with promotion and getting ahead has resulted in a particular conception of management which is aggressive, independent, competitive, ambitious, unemotional and self-confident. This in turn has resulted in a monodimensional interpretation of career. By changing our conception of management to include an ability to express feelings and form empathic relationships with others, as well as being able to be firm and decisive when situations require strong leadership, we might also begin to change our understanding of the 'good' manager as well as of the successful career. When individuals achieve a balance in their lives between career, family and other interests, then career as well as management might prove to be a work-goal worth pursuing. Organizations will also benefit substantially from the extension of management and career opportunities to a larger pool of managerial and administrative talent.

The culture of career and promotion

It is also necessary to recognize that the culture associated with career and promotion success is not gender-neutral. The concepts of merit and promotion are interpreted and operationalized according to a particular model of career success. Merit payments are awarded to those making a distinctive, active contribution to the goals of the work group. But 'active contributions' are differently rated by organizational representatives. Thus, holding particular offices, contributing to professional or organizational development, having specific expertise and needing to be retained are the characteristics deemed worthy of merit awards. Other sorts of characteristics such as stability, long service, organizational loyalty and doing a good job do not in themselves deserve merit. Women *can* earn such awards in the same way as men if they accept the appropriateness of the merit-earning characteristics and are willing to work towards them. However, several reports have demonstrated that merit schemes generally favour men. The trade union representing top civil servants (Association of First Division Civil Servants) has claimed that statistics for the first four years of a new performance-related pay scheme had shown clear gender bias (Whitfield, 1991). There was a consistent pattern of men, on the same grade and with the same seniority, being paid more than women. The decision to award performance-related pay was based on an annual review. People scoring high enough marks were eligible for extra cash but the number actually receiving an award was rationed to a certain percentage of the grade. In the competition for such awards, management discretion was the final arbiter and women received fewer awards than men. In a similar way the Equal Opportunities Commission has argued that even the most 'objective' systems of merit pay and appraisal are likely to apply more readily to jobs performed by men (Industrial Relations Services, 1992). Performance assessments of women's occupations often focused on subjective assessments of attitudes and behaviourial characteristics and casual judgments by line-managers (Clement, 1992b). In these ways the operationalization of merit schemes are not gender-neutral.

In a similar way the operationalization of promotion procedures are also designed to reward only one, unidimensional model of career. There is an assumption in appraisers' and assessors' minds of a linear career track. Frequently there is an assertion of gender-neutrality, an emphasis on 'objective' characteristics and an underlining of the openness of competition. In the rational-legal organization, the focus in promotion decisions is on the human capital characteristics (qualifications, experience) among candidates deemed to be appropriate. In the open competition for promotion posts, the individualistic attributes of candidates are assessed and compared. Past experience is judged and future potential is estimated. But in striving to emphasize achievement characteristics rather than ascription, certain attributes are deemed 'appropriate' whereas others are assumed to be inappropriate. Thus certain pursuits (national service, community position-holders) are rated highly in career terms where as others (raising children, managing households, caring for dependents) count for little. It is also difficult if not impossible for those on promotion panels to separate the job performance from the job holder. Past achievements in jobs will be defined and assessed in relation to the person, male or female, doing the work. Similarly future potential will be appraised in terms of the person. In all these ways gender will intrude in promotion decisions.

Women so far have not been as successful as men in their achievements in hierarchical, linear, competitive career structures in organizations. Some women *are* succeeding. The cost will be high, however, if the unidimensional focus of career and promotion success becomes the only cultural model of career.

Organizational change: career, profession and class

It is critically important to recognize the changes currently under way in work organizations and professions themselves which will inevitably affect the contexts in which careers are constructed. The concepts of 'enterprise culture', 'budgetary devolution' and 'internal markets' have come to represent such changes. Keat has examined the notion of an 'enterprise culture' and this he describes as a radical programme of economic and institutional reform which 'appeals to the efficiency of markets, the liberty of individuals and the non-interventionist state' (Keat and Abercrombie, 1991, p. 1). Budgetary devolution involves the devolving of the responsibility for balancing incomes and expenditures to departments or sections in organizations or to separate units in the provision of services. Control over the budgets themselves is maintained from the centre, however, and what has actually been devolved is a range of accountancy management tasks and budgetary responsibilities. The 'internal market' arises out of budgetary devolution and has had most publicity in respect of publicly funded services such as education and health where service providers are required to compete for clients and cost their services. In organizations, an internal market involves the operation of commercial markets *within* the organization. According to such a model, departments who manage their own budgets are required to 'cost' and to 'sell' their services to other departments in the organization who require them. Thus, within organizations, there are profit- and loss-making departments and sections, as team projects and professional services become internally purchasable commodities.

For individual women and men, whether they work in industrial organizations or professional practices, there are new vocabularies or 'discourses' by means of which professional workers explain and account for their careers. The notion of individual accountability is now commonplace. Professional workers accept appraisal and assessment as a normal part of career development. At (annual) appraisal interviews personal goals are identified, defined according to organizational objectives and progress in respect of such goals is measured, monitored and assessed. This is the new language of career and career promotion.

Organizational scientists and engineers, such as the ones in this study, have always been 'in the market' in the sense that they are employees in large, complex industrial organizations. What has had less attention, however, is how changes in the organization itself and particularly change in systems of management in the organization are affecting careers. In turn, this will have crucially important effects on aspects of the professionalism of organizational scientists and engineers, as well as on wider social class formation and relations. This section considers three related aspects:

1 changes in management and organizations;
2 gender and career in the context of organizational change;
3 careers, class and profession.

Changes in management and organizations

For about 30 years, until the late 1980s, there had been a tremendous growth in managerial posts and positions in industrial, commercial and service organizations as well as in professional and small firm practices. This expansion had been accompanied by other changes such as the increased use of microelectronic equipment in factories, laboratories and offices. A wide variety of work tasks in production, marketing, sales, administration and research and development are now managed by means of reliance on computerized systems and processes.

This expansion in the numbers of managerial posts had also been accompanied by an increased diversification of management positions. Davidson and Cooper (1992) have reported that since 1976, more people occupy management service positions and fewer hold general management jobs. In organizations there is a growing need for technical specialists, but these posts do not include the management of other staff. Many of these so-called 'managers' will be employed in professional consultancy roles that require high levels of very specialized and often organizationally specific technical knowledge. However, these posts will seldom include generalist managerial and administrative responsibility for other employees.

The late 1980s saw a change in the pattern of expansion. In organizations, the upward pressure of the numbers of staff seeking promotion and of heightened expectations for further career development led to the creation of 'surplus' layers of management. The recession in Britain and growing international competition exerted even greater pressure on employers and organizations to contain costs. As a result, whole layers of (particularly junior and middle) management were stripped away; organizations became leaner, flatter systems with more professional specialists but fewer middle and junior managers. The name 'manager' might be retained but such individuals managed a task or a specialist area, not people.

Ways of working were also changing and alongside those changes were marked alterations in employment practices. Ways of working were moving towards more projects that required temporary teams. Individuals would move from one project to another on completion or having completed their contribution. On some projects and in some teams, particular individuals would act as leader but this would not necessarily continue with the move to a different project where they would operate as a team member.

Employment practices also changed and this had dramatic consequences for the experience and expectation of careers. Some permanent employment was replaced by an increase in short-term posts or limited-term contracts. Also, some services previously provided in-house were contracted out and market-testing enabled private companies to bid for work previously managed within organizations. In addition, the creation of departmental budgetary units within organizations enabled profit- and loss-making sections to be more readily identified.

The consequences for the experience of and expectations for careers have been profound. The traditional organizational career had been predictable and made up of variations on the following model: graduate education, joining a company, structured graduate training, a first position and subsequent promotion to a managerial post on the organization's career ladder. The organizational structures with large numbers of middle-manager positions, which enabled such rational career planning, have been changed, however, and future careers might need to be very differently developed. If individuals perform well, they may receive additional pay in the form of merit awards or income supplements, but promotion in the traditional sense, of the next rung on the promotion ladder, will not automatically follow. More professionals who have worked for part of their careers in organizations will become freelance consultants, selling the specialized skills they have developed to firms which need to contract out their knowledge and expertise for particular projects.

Change is then a prominent feature of organizations and their systems of management. The experiences of the women and men scientists and engineers in the careers history study illustrate some of these aspects of change and also demonstrate some of the features of stability and reproduction which are prominent in organizational life.

Gender and career in the context of organizational change

This section will consider how gender, career, management and organization interact in the context of change to produce new as well as to reproduce old forms of occupational segregation and gender differences in careers. Two aspects will be considered. Both have been outlined and illustrated by Savage (1992a). First, his claim is that although women have moved into professional and 'skilled' jobs in the middle classes, they have rarely been able to achieve 'management' positions in the sense of having significant authority in the organization. Second is his claim that the restructuring of organizations themselves, and in particular the rationalization of management in organizations, affects career opportunities and differentially affects the career opportunities of women and men in organizations.

The work of Savage, and of others (see Savage and Witz, Eds, 1992), has emphasized the importance of organizational structures in gender inequality. Savage has also been concerned to emphasize the significance of organizations in class formation, especially middle-class formation, the wider objective being to link the analyses of gender and class inequalities. He has used data on gender and social mobility (the Office of Population Census and Statistics Longitudinal Study) as well as data from his own study of banking (1992b), in order to demonstrate the gender differences in careers. Thus women *have* been entering the professions and developing careers in the sense of achieving promotions in their organization. However, most tend to develop 'occupational' careers, usually within subordinate professional niches. Women have moved into positions of high expertise but not high authority. They have rarely been able to secure positions of managerial authority within hierarchical structures of organizational management.

In respect of the women scientists and engineers in the careers history study, we have seen in previous chapters that some of the women *were* achieving promotions in their organizations. Some of them had attained managerial posts and two had achieved senior managerial positions. Thus women *can* be bureaucrats (Crompton and Le Feuvre, 1992) and develop hierarchical, linear careers. Others were achieving promotion into middle-management posts and, in due course, might anticipate career positions of authority in their organizations.

We need to ask, however, what does 'management' mean in these organizational contexts? Are management posts proliferating? Is management itself diversifying? Is management being significantly changed? As organizations update, down-size and de-layer and management is restructured, should the notion of management itself be rendered problematic in order to enable us to better understand the real significance of management (and gender) in the organization?

Organizational change has also responded to heightened awareness about gender differences in career and promotion positions. Some organizations have promoted a few women to take up 'token positions' (Kanter, 1977) in various departments and levels in the hierarchy (Powell, 1988). Nicholson and West (1988), in a large-scale survey of British Institute Managers members, found that women were following different career paths from men. They were educated to a higher level and were occupying more specialist positions at every level of the managerial hierarchy. Cockburn (1991) analysed recent changes in four organizations (private sector retail trade, a government department, a locally elected council and a national trade union) and the gender consequences of such changes. She evaluated the part played by men in resisting moves to incorporate gender equality in organizational arrangements. One of the organizational responses she described was when women entered management (e.g. in retail stores) the 'real' power had moved elsewhere, to regional centres and headquarters and into the hands of computer programmers, marketing, sales and advertising managers and company accountants, who were male.

Similarly Savage (1992b) catalogued the major restructuring of management in banking organizations. He listed the changes (pp. 141–2) as a diversification away from branch retailing, the streamlining of customer groups, the sub-division of management into 'lending' and 'operations', the development of regional headquarters to deal with the diversified financial services, the controlling of management by means of standardized criteria and annual objectives and a consequent reduction of autonomy and discretion. The effect of such changes has been to greatly increase the numbers of junior categories of management and the numbers of bank employees who have the title 'manager'. A further consequence has been the separation of 'expertise' from 'authority'. Most of these lower-level 'managerial' positions demand high expertise and specialist knowledge but they involve little effective organizational authority within the massively expanded managerial hierarchy.

The growth of women in management in banking has been heralded as a success story. It is claimed that women in banking *are* moving into managerial positions of authority and power. Savage disputes this, however. He claims (1992b, p. 142) that the growth of women in banking management is linked to the changing structure of management itself. Women managers are recruited into positions which demand expertise and skill but they have no effective organizational power; their positions do not involve line-management. Further, he claims that where women *are* employed as managers, they are in units where there are many (often female) managers. In such managerial positions, women remain subordinate to senior, predominantly male, managers.

What, then, were the structures of management at Airmax and Marlands and how were the women 'managers' slotting into those structures? Was there similar evidence of organizational and management restructuring in order to better enable the organizations to compete in national and international markets? And, as a consequence of such organizational requirements, were gendered career patterns emerging, producing (new) and reproducing (old) aspects of occupational segregation in the organizations?

Managerial changes at Airmax were a continuous feature involving turbulent periods of relocation for the engineers as well as periods of readjustment to different job specifications. The rate of change was also increasing. Of particular interest was a major restructuring of management which took place in 1992 *after* the careers history interviews. Prior to 1992, Airmax engineers worked in a fairly traditional departmental system. Departments varied in size and organizational significance but the departments coordinated particular engineering activities such as stress, aerodynamics, thermodynamics, specifications, design, etc. Each department was headed by a manager, an on-line manager, who headed groups of professional engineers (as well as technicians, secretaries and other support staff) and for the larger departments there were significant numbers of team leader positions for particular sections. Every department had its own range of required expertise and skill posts. For a number of years the organization had increased its levels and numbers of management, particularly team leader, positions. The proliferation of management posts had been Airmax's response to the need to motivate and encourage its engineers and to reward them with career and promotion progress.

In 1992, Airmax changed its organization of engineering from a departmental to a project-based system. Change was thereby incorporated into the organization's structure since the idea was that particular projects would be identified and a team would be formed to process the project. On completion, the team would be dissolved or reformulated to deal with other projects. The size of each project team would increase or decrease according to the group's level of activity. Each team would be made up of its own technical specialists who worked with the project as long as their expertise was required.

The explicit intention was to cut the proliferating lower levels of management by converting current post-holders to professional positions. The project teams were to report direct to the chief of a particular technology (a company senior staff position) but in practice a post of project team leader has re-emerged and become established. This is in fact a managerial post although its incumbents occupy professional positions. The result has been that the lower levels of management/supervision have been removed (although some are creeping back). There are team leader positions made up of individuals who organize the project work, although they do not have people reporting to them. They are not on-line managerial posts.

As a result of these changes, all Airmax engineers were regraded and rated according to their expertise not their level of management in the organization. For both women and men engineers at Airmax, a career move into management was made more difficult. Significant managerial responsibilities were not now achieved until chief of particular technology posts, which were company senior staff positions. The (re-appearing) managerial posts of project team leader were temporary (for the life-time of the project) and the job descriptions in fact included no managerial responsibilities.

For the women engineers at Airmax, their positions were especially difficult. They were as able as the men to develop their expertise and skills. But the continuous and single-minded dedication to the organization for long periods of time which was now required for career promotion to chief and head of function positions (company senior staff) constituted a significant hurdle. Only women and men with a single-minded focus on career were likely to climb to this level. In Airmax, there were no women in company senior staff positions. The one woman who was in a director post was single and childfree.

The changes in the organization at Airmax graphically reveal that notions of 'management' itself must be examined, not taken for granted. This also applies to the organization of management at Marlands. In this company the changes were not as far-reaching as at Airmax: Marlands still used the term 'manager' as an indicator of career progression and reward for aspirant scientists. However, Marlands also had changed its organizational system, in this case from a departmental or sectional organization to one which was product-based or process development. Most of the lower-level managerial positions involved managing 'tasks' rather than people and, as such, involved high scientific 'expertise' rather than on-line authority within the organization. Frequently, such management involved no responsibilities for other scientists or technicians.

For the women scientists in the careers history study, these were the management positions most of them were occupying. They were managing tasks rather than people and they were developing their scientific expertise rather than their managerial authority. The sections they were leading had few or no other workers. The four women who were in management posts which were difficult to categorize on the Marlands career structure were in professional-expertise rather than people-management positions.

Careers, class, organization and profession

It has been noted in the previous section how researchers such as Savage, and others (e.g. Savage and Witz, Eds, 1992), have been concerned to emphasize the significance of organizations in class formation as well as in explanations of continuing gender inequalities. The linking of analysis of gender and class has been emphasized, particularly in middle-class formation, development and change.

The concepts of class, profession and organization were examined in Chapter 2. In summary, it can be said that the scientists and engineers under consideration here were salaried professionals and some were aspirant managers; they were part of a middle-class. They worked in industrial organizations; they were 'employees with autonomy, authority, career expectations, a monthly salary, fringe benefits, and a certain security' (Whalley, 1986, p. 185). Professional scientists and engineers working in industry are part of 'trusted labour' or the 'service class' (Goldthorpe, 1982). The links between organizations, class and career have also been emphasized. Thus Goldthorpe (1982, p. 170) described the service class as dependent on 'processes of bureaucratic appointment and achievement'. Others such as Lash and Urry (1987) and Crompton and Le Feuvre (1992) have seen considerable explanatory potential in the concept of an organizational or bureaucratic *career*. Lash and Urry see the development of a career as central to the identification of the service class. In the service class, individuals are bound to their organizations by loyalty in exchange for a career (Goldthorpe, 1982; Abercrombie and Urry, 1983; Lash and Urry, 1987; quoted in Crompton and Le Feuvre, 1992, p. 106).

Organizations are changing, however, and changes are affecting widely understood configurations of organizations, careers and class. The promotion structures which have traditionally sustained rational, long-term career planning, often within one organization, are being replaced by more fluid, perhaps flatter, hierarchies and structures. There is a growing need for specialists in organizations. These might constitute career positions but they require high levels of specialized knowledge and do not, for the most part, involve the 'management' of other staff. Safe and secure bureaucratic, linear and managerial careers within organizations can no longer be assumed or taken for granted.

Social commentators, including journalists, have attempted to assess the political consequences as well as the social effects of such changes. In general such changes have been summed up as an increase in middle-class anxieties and a growing culture of insecurity (Cohen, 1993). In the enterprise culture, the future role for the middle classes is seen to be to become freelance consultants, selling their skills to whichever organization wants to contract their services. Social scientists have, on the whole, been slower to respond with such drastic generalizations and more reluctant to rush to conclusions about comprehensive changes. Models of analysis *have* changed, however, with life-style and consumption classes superseding employment and occupational categories in class theory. In recent analyses, the 'new middle class' is a prominent category (e.g. Crompton, 1993) with distinctive (and privileged) lifestyles, cultural and symbolic capital and educational and social opportunities, rather than a privileged employment or professional grouping.

It is now very difficult, if not impossible, for writers and researchers on class to ignore the gender dimensions of class reproduction and change, although such an omission had been commonplace in analyses until the 1980s. The part played by women in the family-related aspects of class, as well as in the work places and in organizations and professions, have become an essential component of class theory. Researchers have begun to demonstrate, sometimes using historical data, how gender segregation within organizations and professions has enabled men to progress in their careers while women continued to do the backstage work. There is, then, a reforming division of labour in work in organizations, which mirrors that in other professions and occupations and is part of the process of middle-class change and development more generally.

The changes in organizations themselves play an important part in this reformulation. Savage (1992a) has noted that skill assets are less intrinsically gendered: both successful women and men use skill assets. But whereas women are dependent on skill assets, men are not. Men also use organizational assets, since promotion processes are important vehicles of male power (Hearn *et al.*, Eds, 1989). When women use their skill assets in their careers they become professional specialists according to the organization's changed requirements. But their very specialization then renders them ill-equipped and ill-experienced for positions of general management in the organization. Organizations have changed their management requirements. Both women and men have had to respond, but positions of power and authority in the organization are still predominantly retained for men.

Bureaucracy and organizations result in different outcomes for men's and women's careers even when the women and men are doing similar work. It is important to emphasize, however, that there is considerable variation among women and among men. The postmodernist shift in social thought (Crompton, 1993) requires the incorporation of cultural as well as structural dimensions and a consideration of the diversity and variety of experiences alongside generalized conceptions of stability and change. Thus women can and some do develop bureaucratic promotional careers in organizations; some, but not all, remain childfree, calculate promotion moves and progress up linear-career hierarchies. Even for women such as these, however, their gender often remains critical in their experiences of career. They become *women* managers or even *women* directors and their gender continues to be important and implicit in the ways they are perceived and particularly assessed by others. Thus, cultural modes and patterns continue to reinforce traditional aspects of organizational structures as well as generating diversities in experience which might feature in organizational change.

Finally, it is necessary to include some of the wider aspects of profession alongside class and organization as contexts in which corporate science and engineering careers are constructed. In Chapter 2, these were discussed as the macro-level processes of professional competition that operate within and between organizations and professions at both nation-state and increasingly at international levels. Abbott's work on a system model of professions was considered which emphasized professions' interrelations and competition over jurisdictions. Such competitions brought the professions into conflict with each other as well as making their histories interdependent (Abbott, 1988, p. 19). The experiences of the scientists and engineers in this study make it clear that it is not only control of work that brings the professions into competition and conflict but also competition over career. This is particularly prevalent in professional careers constructed in organizations where an interprofessional division of labour and a legally protected market shelter (Freidson, 1983, 1994) are replaced by an intra-organizational and more pragmatic division of tasks and responsibilities.

In organizations, most professional jurisdictional competitions are competitions about career. Competition over control of work in the work place, over control of new technology or scientific development, or of professional rivalries within organizations, can be perceived as competitions about promotion, increased authority, status and income in the organization. New areas of career competition are also developing, this time between women and men and within families in addition to those within the organizations themselves. In the career competitions between women and men in organizations, women have been at a disadvantage in respect of the cultural, structural and action dimensions of career. However, there are an increasing number of partnerships where both partners are in the same or very similar professional fields. Traditionally women have supported and backed their partners in competitions in the organization over careers and promotions. This might not continue, however, if women, like their partners, see themselves as serious competitors in the race for careers. In this way career needs to be included in theoretical models and explanations alongside class, profession and gender in the analysis of culture, structure and action dimensions of organizations.

Conclusion

Alongside and interrelated with all the previously considered variables and dimensions of career is the additional complexity of gender. The operation of class, organizational and professional dimensions affect the careers of women in different ways to those of men, though there are also wide variations in experience within the gender categories. For a long time the private and public dimensions of career were separated both in theory and in empirical research. This resulted in not only incomplete but also inaccurate understandings about the processes of class, profession and organization on careers. Analysis is of necessity changing and gender has been demonstrated to be a critical variable in the culture, structure and action dimensions of career, as well as of social change more generally (MacEwen Scott, 1994).

It is important to end by restating the principle of structuration which has been critical in this analysis: of how career structures and cultures emerge and are reproduced or changed by career actions. The structural and cultural determinants of and constraints on careers and promotions are real and formidable. But career actions *can* alter structures and eventually cultures, just as structures affect and constrain career actions.

We need to understand, therefore, the complex processes which are cultural and structural and which are also political (legislative changes and ideological beliefs) as well as functional and strategic (changes in job descriptions for particular positions). These are the processes that constrain and limit career action so that career structures become real. Careers are normative in that they are constraining and limit choices of action. But careers are also cognitive in that they are understood, experienced and used (Knorr-Cetina and Cicourel, Eds, 1981). By analysing the processes of change in organizations, professions and careers, we can have such interrelations between culture, structure and action constantly in mind. Only by beginning to understand how change provides opportunities as well as constraints can we begin to devise career actions that will be appropriate for changing career structures.

References

ABBOTT, A. (1988) *The System of Professions: an Essay on the division of Expert Labour*, Chicago: University of Chicago Press.

ABBOTT, P. and SAPSFORD, R. (1987) *Women and Social Class*, London: Tavistock.

ABERCROMBIE, N. and URRY, J. (1983) *Capital, Labour and the Middle Classes*, London: Allen & Unwin.

ABRAMS, P. (1982) *Historical Sociology*, Shepton Mallet: Open Books.

ACKER, S. (1980) 'Women, the other academics', *British Journal of Sociology of Education*, **1**, 1, pp. 68-80.

ACKER, S. (1989) (Ed.) *Teachers, Gender and Careers*, Lewes: Falmer Press.

ADAMS, C. T. and WINSTON, K. T. (1980) *Mothers at Work: Public Policies in the US, Sweden and China*, New York and London: Longman.

ALDRIDGE, A. (1994) 'Whose service is perfect freedom: women's careers in the Church of England' in Evetts, J. (Ed.) *Women and Career: Themes and Issues in Advanced Industrial Societies*, London: Longman.

ALLATT, P. (1986) 'The young unemployed: independence and identity' in Pashley, B. (Ed.) *Youth Unemployment and the Transition to Adulthood*, papers in Social Policy and Professional Studies, Hull: University of Hull.

ALLEN, S. (1986) *The Experience of Unemployment*, London: Macmillan.

ATKINSON, P. (1983) 'The reproduction of professional community' in Dingwall, R. and Lewis, P. (Eds) *Sociology of the Professions: Doctors, Lawyers and Others*, London: Macmillan.

ATKINSON, P. and DELAMONT, S. (1990) 'Professions and powerlessness: female marginality in the learned occupations', *Sociological Review*, **38**, 1, pp. 90–110.

BACCHI, C. (1990) *Same Difference: Feminism and Sexual Difference*, Sydney: Allen & Unwin.

BADINTER, E. (1982) *The Myth of Motherhood*, London: Souvenir Press.

BALL, S. J. (1987) *The Micro-Politics of the School*, London and New York: Methuen.

BANKS, M., BATES. I., BREAKWELL, G., BYNNER, J., EMLER, N., JAMIESON, L. and ROBERTS, K. (1992) *Careers and Identities*, Milton Keynes: Open University Press.

BARKER, D. L. and ALLEN, S. (Eds) (1976) *Dependence and Exploitation in Work and Marriage*, London: Longman.

BATES, I. (1990) 'No bleeding whining minnies: the role of YTS in class and gender reproduction', *British Journal of Education and Work*, **3**, pp. 91–110.

BECKER, H. S. (1963) *Outsiders: Studies in the Sociology of Deviance*, Chicago: Free Press.

BECKER, H. S., GEER, B., HUGHES, E. C. and STRAUSS, A. L. (1961) *Boys in White*, Chicago: University of Chicago Press.

BEECHEY, V. (1987) *Unequal Work*, London: Verso.

BERGER, M., FOSTER, M. A. and WALLSTON, B. S. (1978) 'I will follow him: myth, reality or forced choice? Job-seeking experiences of dual-career couples', *Psychology of Women Quarterly*, **3**, pp. 9–21.

BERTAUX, D. (1981) *Biography and Society*, London: Sage.

BEYNON, J. (1985) 'Institutional change and career histories in a comprehensive school', in Ball, S. J. and Goodson, I. F. (Eds) *Teachers' Lives and Careers*, pp. 158–79, Lewes: Falmer Press.

BLACKSTONE, T. and WEINREICH-HASTE, H. (1980) 'Why are there so few women scientists and engineers?', *New Society*, **51**, pp. 383–5.

BOLTANSKI, L. (1987) *The Making of a Class, Cadres in French Society*, Cambridge: University Press.

BOURDIEU, P. (1986) *Distinction: a Social Critique of the Judgment of Taste*, London: Routledge.

BOURDIEU, P. (1987) 'What makes a social class?', *Berkeley Journal of Sociology*, **22**, pp. 1–18.

BOURDIEU, P. (1988) *Homo Academicus*, Oxford: Polity Press.

BOURDIEU, P. and WACQUANT, L. (1992) *An Invitation to Reflexive Sociology*, Cambridge: Polity Press.

BOURNE, P. and WIKLER, N. (1982) 'Commitment and the cultural mandate: women in medicine' in Kahn-Hut, R., Kaplan-Daniels, A. and Colvard, R. (Eds) *Women and Work: Problems and Perspectives*, Oxford: Oxford University Press.

BRANNEN, J. and MOSS, P. (1991) *Managing Mothers: Dual Earner Households after Maternity Leave*, London: Unwin Hyman.

BRAYBON, G. (1981) *Women Workers in the First World War: the British Experience*, London: Croom Helm.

BREAKWELL, G. M. (1986) 'Identities at work' in Beloff, H. (Ed.) *Getting into Life*, London: Methuen.

BREAKWELL, G. M., COLLIE, A., HARRISON, B. and PROPFER, C. (1984) 'Attitudes towards the unemployed: effects of threatened identity', *British Journal of Social Psychology*, **23**, pp. 87-8.

BROWN, R. (1982) 'Work histories, career structures and class structure', in Giddens, A. and MacKenzie, G. (Eds) *Social Class and the Division of Labour*, Cambridge: Cambridge University Press.

BRUBAKER, R. (1985) 'Rethinking classical theory', *Theory and Society*, **14**, pp. 745–73.

BYRNE, E. (1978) *Women and Education*, London: Tavistock.

BYRNE, E. (1993) *Women and Science: the Snark Syndrome*, London: The Falmer Press.

CARTER, A. and KIRKUP, G. (1990) *Women in Engineering*, Basingstoke: Macmillan.

CHODOROW, N. (1978) *The Reproduction of Mothering: Psychoanalysis and the Sociology of Gender*, Berkeley: University of California Press.

CLEGG, S. (1989) *Power and its Foundations*, London: Sage.

CLEMENT, B. (1992a) 'Bias in selection keeps women out of top jobs', *Independent*, 8 January 1992, p. 4.

CLEMENT, B. (1992b) 'Merit pay schemes favour men', *Independent*, 8 July 1992 p. 2.

CLEMENT, B. and MACINTYRE, D. (1993) 'Employers prepare to ditch equal opportunities at work', *Independent on Sunday*, 14 February 1993, p. 1.

COATES, J. (1986) *Women, Men and Language*, London: Longman

COCKBURN, C. (1985) *Machinery of Dominance*, London: Pluto Press.

COCKBURN, C. (1991) *In the Way of Women*, Basingstoke: Macmillan.

COFFEE, A. and ATKINSON, P. (Eds) (1994) *Occupational Socialization and Working Lives*, Aldershot: Avebury.

COHEN, D. (1990) *Being a Man*, London: Routledge.

COHEN, N. (1993) 'Nobody is safe', *Independent on Sunday*, 24 October 1993, p. 17.

COLE, J. (1979) *Fair Science: Women in the Scientific Community*, New York: Free Press.

COLLINS, R. (1979) *The Credential Society*, Orlando, Florida: Academic Press.

COLLINS, R. (1981) 'Micro-translation as a theory-building strategy' in Knorr-Cetina, K. and Cicourel, A. V. (Eds) *Advances in Social Theory and Methodology*, Boston, London and Henley: Routledge & Kegan Paul.

COLLINSON, D. and KNIGHTS, D. (1986) ' "Men only": theories and practices of job segregation in insurance' in Knights, D. and Collinson, C. (Eds) *Gender and the Labour Process*, Aldershot: Gower.

CORRADI, C. (1991) 'Text, context and individual meaning: rethinking life histories in a hermeneutic framework', *Discourse and Society*, **2**, 1, pp. 105–18.

CROMPTON, R. (1986) 'Women and the service class', in Crompton, R. and Mann, M. (Eds) *Gender and Stratification*, Cambridge: Polity Press.

CROMPTON, R. (1993) *Class and Stratification: an Introduction to Current Debates*, Cambridge: Polity Press.

CROMPTON, R. and LE FEUVRE, N. (1992) 'Gender and bureaucracy: women in finance in Britain and France', in Savage, M. and Witz, A. (Eds) *Gender and Bureaucracy*, Oxford: Blackwell.

CROMPTON, R. and SANDERSON, K. (1990) *Gendered Jobs and Social Change*, London: Unwin Hyman.

CROW, G. (1989) 'The use of the concept of "strategy" in the recent sociological literature', *Sociology*, **23**, 1, pp. 1–24.

DANIEL, W. W. (1987) *Workplace Industrial Relations and Technical Change*, London: Frances Pinter in association with the Policy Studies Institute.

DAVIDSON, M. J. and COOPER, C. L. (1983) *Stress and the Woman Manager*, London: Martin Robertson.

DAVIDSON, M. J. and COOPER, C. L. (1992) *Shattering the Glass Ceiling: the Woman Manager*, London: Paul Chapman Publishing.

Department of Education and Science (1985) *Science 5-16: a Statement of Policy*, London: HMSO.

DEX, S. (1985) *The Sexual Division of Work*, Brighton: Wheatsheaf.

DEX, S. (1988) *Women's Attitudes to Work*, London: Macmillan.

DEX, S. and SHAW, L. (1986) *British and American Women at Work*, London: Macmillan.

DEX, S. and WALTERS, P. (1989) 'Women's occupational status in Britain, France and USA: explaining the difference', *Industrial Relations Journal*, **20**, 3, pp. 203-12, Autumn.

DINGWALL, R. and LEWIS, P. (Eds) (1983) *The Sociology of the Professions: Doctors, Lawyers and Others*, London: Macmillan.

EDGELL, S. (1980) *Middle-Class Couples*, London: Allen and Unwin.

ELIAS, P. and RIGG, M. (Eds) (1990) *The Demand for Graduates*, London: Policy Studies Institute and Institute for Employment Research.

ENLOE, C. (1983) *Khaki Becomes You*, London: Pluto Press.

EVANS, S. M. (1989) *Born for Liberty: a History of Women in America*, New York: Free Press.

EVETTS, J. (1990) *Women in Primary Teaching*, London: Unwin Hyman.

EVETTS, J. (1992) 'Dimensions of career: avoiding reification in the analysis of change', *Sociology*, **26**, pp. 1-26.

EVETTS, J. (1993) 'Careers and partnerships: the strategies of secondary headteachers', *The Sociological Review*, **41**, 2, pp. 302-27.

EVETTS, J. (1994a) (Ed.) *Women and Career: Themes and Issues in Advanced Industrial Societies*, London: Longman.

EVETTS, J. (1994b) *Becoming a Secondary Headteacher*, London: Cassell.

EVETTS, J. (1994c) 'Gender and career in engineering and science: changing management in the organization', presentation at ISA Conference, Bielefeld, July.

FAGENSON, E. (Ed.) (1993) *Women in Management*, London: Sage.

FARADAY, A. and PLUMMER, K. (1979) 'Doing life histories', *Sociological Review*, **27**, 4, pp. 773-93.

FARGANIS, S. (1986) *The Social Reconstruction of the Feminine Character*, Totowa, New Jersey: Rowman & Littlefield.

FEE, E. (1981) 'Is feminism a threat to scientific objectivity?', *Journal of College Science Teaching*, **11**, 2, pp. 84–92.

FERBER, M. A., O'FARRELL, B. and LA RUE, A. (Eds) (1991) *Work and Family*, Washington DC: National Academic Press.

FINCH, J. (1983) *Married to the Job*, London: Allen & Unwin.

FINCH, J. and GROVES, D. (Eds) (1983) *A Labour of Love: Women, Work and Caring*, London: Routledge & Kegan Paul.

FINNISTON, M. (1980) *Engineering our Future*, Report of the Committee of Engineering into the Engineering Profession, London: HMSO, Dept of Industry, Cmnd 7794.

FIRTH-COZENS, J. and WEST, M. (Eds) (1991) *Women at Work*, Milton Keynes: Open University Press.

FREIDSON, E. (1983) 'The theory of professions', in Dingwall, R. and Lewis, P. (Eds) *The Sociology of the Professions*, London: St Martins.

FREIDSON, E. (1994) *Professionalism Reborn*, Cambridge: Polity Press.

GERSHUNY, J. I. (1983) *Social Innovation and the Division of Labour*, Oxford: Oxford University Press.

GIDDENS, A. (1984) *The Constitution of Society*, Cambridge: Polity Press.

GILLIGAN, C. (1982) *In a Different Voice*, Cambridge: Harvard University Press.

GLASER, B. G. and STRAUSS, A. L. (1967) *The Discovery of Grounded Theory*, Chicago: Aldine.

GLAZER, P. N. and SLATER, M. (1987) *Unequal Colleagues: the Entrance of Women into the Professions 1890–1940*, New Brunswick, N.J.: Rutgers University Press.

GOFFMAN, E. (1968) *Asylums*, Harmondsworth: Penguin.

GOFFMAN, E. (1969) *The Presentation of Self in Everyday Life*, Harmondsworth: Penguin.

GOLDSMITH, E. (Ed.) (1989) *Work and Family*, London and Newbury Park, Cal.: Sage.

GOLDTHORPE, J. H. (1982) 'On the service class, its formations and future', in Giddens, A. and MacKenzie, G. (Eds) *Social Class and the Division of Labour*, Cambridge: Cambridge University Press.

GOODSON, I. (1981) 'Life histories and the study of schooling', *Interchange*, (Canada) **11**, 4, pp. 62–76.

GOODSON, I. (1983) 'The use of life histories in the study of teaching', in Hammersley, M. (Ed.) *The Ethnography of Schooling*, pp. 129–54, Driffield: Nafferton.

GOODSON, I. (1991) 'Teachers' lives and educational research', in Goodson, I. and Walker, R. (Eds) *Biography, Identity and Schooling: Episodes in Educational Research*, pp. 137–49, Lewes: Falmer Press.

GRAY, B. (1994) 'Women-only management training – a past and present', in Tanton, M. *Women in Management*, London: Routledge.

GRAY, H. L. (1987) 'Gender considerations in school management', *School Organisation*, **7**, 3, pp. 297–302.

GREGSON, N. and LOWE, M. (1994) 'Waged domestic labour and the renegotiation of the domestic division of labour with dual career households', *Sociology*, **28**, 1, pp. 55–78.

GRIFFIN, C. (1985) *Typical Girls? Young Women from School to the Full-time Job Market*, London: Routledge & Kegan Paul.

GUNZ, H. (1989) 'The dual meaning of managerial careers: organizational and individual levels of analysis', *Journal of Management Studies*, **26**, pp. 225–50.

HACKER, S. (1989) *Pleasure, Power and Technology*, London: Unwin Hyman.

HACKER, S. (1990) *Doing It the Hard Way*, London: Unwin Hyman.

HALFORD, S. (1992) 'Feminist change in a patriarchal organization', in Savage, M. and Witz, W. (Eds) *Gender and Bureaucracy*, Oxford: Blackwell.

Hansard Society Commission (1990) *Women at the Top*, London: Hansard Society.

HARTSOCK, N. (1983) *Money, Sex and Power*, New York: Longman.

HEARN, J., SHEPPARD, D., TANCRED-SHERIFF, P. and BURRELL, G. (Eds) (1989) *The Sexuality of Organisations*, London: Sage.

HERBERT, S. G. and YOST, E. B. (1979) 'Women as effective managers: a strategic model for overcoming the barriers', *Human Resource Management*, **17**, pp. 18–25.

HIRSH, W. and JACKSON, C. (1989) *Women into Management: Issues Reflecting the Entry of Women into Managerial Jobs*, Paper no. 158, University of Sussex: Institute of Manpower Studies.

HUGHES, E. C. (1937) 'Institutional office and the person', *American Journal of Sociology* **43**, pp. 404–13.

HUGHES, E. C. (1958) *Men and their Work*, New York: Free Press.

HURRELMANN, K. (1988) *Social Structure and Personality Development*, Cambridge: Cambridge University Press.

Industrial Relations Services (1992) *Pay and Gender in Britain 2*, London: Industrial Relations Services.

Institute for Employment Research (1988) *Review of the Economy and Employment: Occupation Studies*, Warwick: University of Warwick.

Institute of Management (1992) *The Key to the Men's Club*, Bristol: I. M. Books.

Institute of Management Survey (1994) *National Management Salary Survey*, Bristol.

Institute of Managers and Remuneration Economics (1993) *National Management Salary Survey*, Kingston-upon-Thames: Remuneration Economics.

JACKSON, J. A. (Ed.) (1970) *Professions and Professionalisation*, Cambridge: Cambridge University Press.

JENSON, J., HAGEN, E. and REDDY, C. (Eds) (1988) *Feminisation of the Labour Force: Paradoxes and Promises*, Cambridge: Polity Press.

JOHNSON, M. (1983) 'Professional careers and biographies', in Dingwall, R. and Lewis, P. (Eds) *The Sociology of the Professions*, London: Macmillan.

JOHNSON, T. (1972) *Professions and Power*, London: Macmillan.

KAMINSKI, D. M. (1982) 'Girls and mathematics: an annotated bibliography of British work 1970–81', *Studies in Science Education*, **9**, pp. 81–108.

KANTER, R. M. (1977) *Men and Women of the Corporation*, New York: Basic Books.

KEAT, R. and ABERCROMBIE, N. (1991) *Enterprise Culture*, London: Routledge.

KELLER, E. FOX, (1982) 'Feminism and science', *SIGNS*, **7**, 3, Spring, pp 589–602.

KELLY, A. (1981) *The Missing Half: Girls and Science Education*, Manchester: Manchester University Press.

KELLY, A. (Ed.) (1987) *Science for Girls?*, Milton Keynes: Open University Press.

KING, M. (1994) 'Women's careers in academic science: achievement and recognition' in Evetts, J. (Ed.) *Women and Career: Themes and Issues in Advanced Industrial Societies*, London: Longman.

KLEIN, V. (1972) *The Feminine Character: History of an Ideology*, Urbana: University of Illinois Press.

KNIGHT, J. and PRITCHARD, S. (1994) 'Women's development programmes – "No, we're not colour consultants!"' Tanton, M. (Ed.) *Women in Management*, London: Routledge.

KNORR-CETINA, K. and CICOUREL, A. V. (Eds) (1981) *Advances in Social Theory and Methodology*, Boston, London and Henley: Routledge & Kegan Paul.

KUHN, A. and WOLPE, A. M. (Eds) (1978) *Feminism and Materialism*, Boston and Henley: Routledge.

LACEY, C. (1977) *The Socialization of Teachers*, London: Methuen.

LASH, S. and URRY, J. (1987) *The End of Organized Capitalism*, Cambridge: Polity Press.

LAWN, M. and OZGA, J. (1981) *Teachers, Professionalism and Class*, Lewes: Falmer Press.

LAWN, M. and GRACE, G. (Eds) (1987) *Teachers: the Culture and Politics of Work*, Lewes: Falmer Press

MACEWEN SCOTT, A. (1994) *Gender and Segregation and Social Change*, Oxford: Oxford University Press.

MARSHALL, J. (1984) *Women Managers: Travellers in a Male World*, Chichester: John Wiley & Sons.

MARTIN, J. and ROBERTS, C. (1984) *Women and Employment: a Lifetime Perspective*, London: HMSO.

McKINLAY, J. B. (1982) 'Towards the proletarianisation of physicians' in Derber, C. (Ed.) *Professionals as Workers*, Boston: G. K Hall.

McKINLAY, J. B. and ARCHES, J. (1985) 'Towards the proletarianisation of physicians', *International Journal of Health Services*, **15**.

McLOUGHLIN, I. and CLARK, F. (1988) *Technological Change at Work*, Milton Keynes: Open University Press.

McRae, S. (1986) *Cross-Class Families: a Study of Wives' Occupational Superiority*, Oxford: Clarendon Press.

McRae, S. (1991) 'Occupational change over childbirth: evidence from a national survey', *Sociology*, **25**, 4, pp. 589–605.

McRae, S., Devine, F. and Lakey, J. (1991) *Women into Science and Engineering*, London: Policy Studies Institute.

McRobbie, A. (1978) 'Working-class girls and the culture of femininity' in *Women Take Issue*, Centre for Contemporary Cultural Studies: University of Birmingham.

Miller, N. and Morgan, D. (1993) 'Called to account: the CV as an autobiographical practice', *Sociology*, **27**, 1, pp. 133–43.

Mitchell, J. C. (1983) 'Case and situation analysis', *Sociological Review*, **31**, pp. 187–211.

Morgan, D. (1986) *Images of Organisations*, London: Sage.

Morrison, A. M. and Von Glinow, M. A. (1990) 'Women and minorities in management', *American Psychologist*, **45**, 2, pp. 200–8.

Moss, P. and Fonda, N. (Eds) (1980) *Work and Family*, London: Temple Smith.

Murphy, R. (1990) 'Proletarianisation or bureaucratisation: the fall of the professional?', in Torstendahl, R. and Burrage, M. (Eds) *The Formation of Professions: Knowledge, State and Strategy*, pp. 71–96, London: Sage.

Myrdal, A. and Klein, V. (1968) *Women's Two Roles*, London: Routledge & Kegan Paul.

Newman, J. (1991) 'Enterprising women: images of success', in Franklin, S. *et al.* (Eds) *Off-Centre Feminism and Cultural Studies*, London: HarperCollins Academic.

Nicholson, N. and West, M. A. (1988) *Managerial Job Change: Men and Women in Transition*, Cambridge: Cambridge University Press.

OECD (1986) *Girls and Women in Education*, Paris, OECD.

Parkin, F. (1974) 'Strategies of social closure in class formation', in Parkin, F. (Ed.) *The Social Analysis of Class Structure*, London: Tavistock.

Pateman, C. (1988) *The Sexual Contract*, Oxford: Polity Press.

Pfeffer, J. (1989) 'A political perspective on careers: interests, networks and environments', in Arthur, M. B. *et al.* (Eds) *Handbook of Career Theory*, Cambridge: University Press.

Pilcher, J., Delamont, S., Powell, G. and Rees, T. (1988) 'Women's training roadshows and the manipulation of schoolgirls' career choices', *British Journal of Education and Work*, **2**, 2, pp. 61–6.

Podmore, D. and Spencer, A. (1986) 'Gender in the labour process – the case of women and men lawyers', in Knights, D. and Willmott, H. (Eds) *Gender and the Labour Process*, London: Gower.

Powell, G. N. (1988) *Women and Men in Management*, Newbury Park and London: Sage.

Pratt, J., Bloomfield, J. and Seale, C. (1984) *Option Choice*, Windsor: NFER-Nelson.

PRINGLE, R. (1989) *Secretaries Talk: Sexuality, Power and Work*, London: Verso.

REES, T. (1992) *Women and the Labour Market*, London: Routledge.

RICH, A. (1976) *Of Woman Born*, New York: W.W. Norton.

ROPER, M. and TOSH, J. (Eds) (1991) *Manful Assertions*, London: Routledge.

RUBERY, J., HORRELL, S. and BURCHELL, B. (1994) 'Part-time work and gender inequality in the labour market', in MacEwen Scott, A. (Ed.) *Gender Segregation and Social Change*, Oxford: Oxford University Press.

SARGENT, A. (1981) *The Androgynous Manager*, New York: AMACOM.

SAVAGE, M. (1992a) 'Women's expertise, men's authority: gendered organisation and the contemporary middle classes', in Savage, M. and Witz, A. (Eds) *Gender and Bureaucracy*, Oxford: Blackwell.

SAVAGE, M. (1992b) 'Gender and career mobility in banking 1880–1940', in Miles, A. and Vincent, D. (Eds) *Building European Society*, Manchester: Manchester University Press.

SAVAGE, M. and WITZ, A. (1992) (Eds) *Gender and Bureaucracy*, Oxford: Blackwell.

SCANZONI, J. (1978) *Sex Roles, Women's Work and Marital Conflict*, Lexington, Mass., DC: Heath & Co.

SCASE, R. and GOFFEE, R. (1989) *Reluctant Managers*, London: Unwin Hyman.

SCHOFIELD, P. (1993) 'Move sideways and get ahead', *Independent*, 9 September 1993, p. 28.

SCHWARZ-COWAN, R. (1979) 'From Virginia Dare to Virginia Slims: women and technology in American life', *Technology and Culture*, **20**, January.

SCOTT, J. (1986) 'Gender: a useful category of historical analysis', *American Historical Review*, **91**, pp. 1053–75.

SEIDLER, V. J. (1989) *Rediscovering Masculinity*, London: Routledge.

SEKARAN, U. and LEONG, F. T. L. (1992) *Womanpower: Managing in Times of Demographic Turbulance*, London, Sage.

SHAKESHAFT, C. (1979) 'Dissertation research on women in educational administration: a synthesis of findings and paradigm for future research', *Dissertation Abstracts International*, **40**, 6455a.

SHAKESHAFT, C. (1985) 'Strategies for overcoming the barriers to women in educational administration', in Klein, S. (Ed.) *Handbook for Achieving Sexequity through Education*, pp. 124–44, John Hopkins University Press.

SHAKESHAFT, C. (1987) *Women in Educational Administration*, Beverley Hills and London: Sage.

SHARPE, S. (1976) *Just Like a Girl*, Harmondsworth: Penguin

SHARPE, S. (1984) *Double Identity*, Harmondsworth: Penguin

SHEPPARD, D. (1989) 'Organizations, power and sexuality: the image and self-image of women managers', in Hearn, J., Sheppard, D., Tancred-Sheriff, P. and Burrell, G. (Eds) *The Sexuality of Organization*, London: Sage.

SHERRATT, N. (1983) 'Girls, jobs and glamour', *Feminist Review,* **15**, pp. 47–61.

SIKES, P., MEASOR, L. and WOODS, P. (1985) *Teacher Careers*, Lewes: Falmer Press.

SILVERSTONE, R. and WARD, A. (1980) *Careers of Professional Women*, London: Croom Helm.

SLOCUM, W. L. (1966) *Occupational Careers: a Sociological Perspective*, Chicago: Aldine.

SMAIL, B., WHYTE, J. and KELLY, A. (1982) 'Girls in science and technology: the first two years', *Social Science Review*, June, pp. 620-30.

SMITH, C. (1990) 'How are engineers formed? Professionals, nation and class politics', *Work, Employment and Society*, **3**, 4, pp. 451–70.

Social Trends (1994), London: HMSO.

SPENCER, A. and PODMORE, D. (1987) (Eds) *In a Man's World*, London: Tavistock.

STANWORTH, M. (1983) *Gender and Schooling: a Study of Sexual Divisions in the Classroom*, London: Hutchinson.

STEBBINS, R. A. (1970) 'Careers: the subjective approach', *Sociological Quarterly*, pp. 32–49.

STRAUSS, A. L. (1977) *Mirrors and Masks: the Search for Identity*, London: Martin Robertson.

STRAUSS, A. L. and BECKER, H. S. (1975) 'Careers, personality and adult socialisation', in Strauss, A. L. (Ed.) *Professions, Work and Careers*, New Brunswick, N.J.: Transaction Books.

SUMMERFIELD, P. (1989) *Women Workers in the Second World War: Production and Patriarchy in Conflict*, London: Routledge.

TANTON, M. (Ed.) (1994) *Women in Management: a Developing Presence*, London: Routledge.

TAYLOR, L. and COHEN, S. (1972) *Psychological Survival*, Harmondsworth: Penguin.

THOMAS, K. (1990) *Gender and Subject in Higher Education*, Buckingham: Society for Research in Higher Education and Open University Press.

THOMPSON, C. A., THOMAS C. C. and MAIER, M. (1992) 'Work-family conflict: reassessing corporate policies and initiatives', in Sekaran, U. and Leong, F. (Eds) *Womanpower*, Newbury Park and London: Sage.

WAJCMAN, J. (1994) 'The gender relations of management', paper presented at *Work, Employment and Society* Conference, September 1994.

WEBER, M. (1948) 'Bureaucracy', in Gerth, H. and Mills, C. W. (Eds) *From Max Weber*, London: Routledge & Kegan Paul.

WEBER, M. (1968) *Economy and Society: an Outline of Interpretive Sociology*, translated by Roth, G. and Wittich, G., New York: Bedminster Press.

WHALLEY, P. (1986) *The Social Production of Technical Work: the Case of British Engineers*, London: Macmillan

WHITE, B., COX, C. and COOPER, C. (1992) *Women's Career Development: a Study of High Flyers*, Oxford, Basil Blackwell.

WHITFIELD, M. (1991) 'Civil servants claim sex bias in pay system', *Independent*, 4 September 1991, p. 5.

WILENSKY, H. L. (1960) 'Work, careers and social integration', *International Social Science Journal*, **12**. Reprinted in Burns, T. (1969) *Industrial Man*, Harmondsworth: Penguin.

WILLIAMS, C. L. (1992) 'The glass escalator: hidden advantages for men in 'female" professions', *Social Problems*, **39**, 3, pp. 253–68.

WILLIS, P. E. (1977) *Learning to Labour*, Aldershot: Saxon House.

WILSON, F. M. (1995) *Organisational Behaviour and Gender*, London: McGraw-Hill.

WITZ, A. (1988) 'Patriarchal relations and patterns of sex segregation in the medical division of labour', in Walby, S. (Ed.) *Gender Segregation at Work*, Milton Keynes: Open University Press.

WITZ, A. (1990) 'Patriarchy and professions: the gendered politics of occupational closure', *Sociology*, **24**, 4, pp. 675–90.

WITZ, A. (1992) *Professions and Patriarchy*, London: Routledge.

WRIGHT, E. O. (1985) *Classes*, London: Verso.

YEANDLE, S. (1984) *Women's Working Lives*, London: Tavistock.

YOUNG, M. and WILLMOTT, P. (1973) *The Symmetrical Family*, London: Routledge & Kegan Paul.

ZUSSMAN, R. (1985) *Mechanics of the Middle Class: Work and Politics among American Engineers*, London: University of California Press.

Index